The Jews of Silence

ELIE WIESEL

The Jews of Silence

A Personal Report on Soviet Jewry

Translated from the Hebrew by Neal Kozodoy

With a New Preface by Elie Wiesel
and a New Afterword by Martin Gilbert

SCHOCKEN BOOKS/NEW YORK

First Schocken paperback edition 1987

10 9 8 7 6 5 4 3 2 1   87 88 89 90

Library of Congress Cataloging-in-Publication Data
Wiesel, Elie, 1928–
The Jews of silence.
Translation of: Les juifs du silence.
"Originally written as a series of articles for
the Israeli newspaper, Yediot Aharanot"—Copr. p.
1. Jews—Soviet Union—Persecutions. 2. Wiesel,
Elie, 1928– —Journeys—Soviet Union. 3. Soviet
Union—Description and travel—1945–1969. 4. Soviet
Union—Ethnic relations. 5. Jewish authors—
Journeys—Soviet Union. I. Title.
DS135.R92W5313 1987   305.8'924'047   86-26134

Design by Cassandra Pappas
Manufactured in the United States of America
ISBN 0–8052–0826–7

CONTENTS

PREFACE TO THE THIRD EDITION

Martin Gilbert calls them "the Jews of Hope." He is right. Their hope is both stunning and contagious. Their hope is a justification of our own. Should they give up on their Jewishness and ours, we would never be forgiven.

This I felt during my first journey to Russia in 1965; during my second one and my third one, too. Russian Jewry wants to remain an integral and inherent part of the Jewish people. For this they are ready to pay the highest price, that of their freedom.

Have things changed since 1965? Yes, they have. In 1965, no one dared to dream of legal emigration to Israel and other free countries. Now it is no longer a dream. Now it has become a political situation that demands political remedies. What happened in the late 1970s could very well happen again: the gates may open for all those Refuseniks* whose only wish is to join their families in Israel.

Otherwise, my report of 1965 has remained valid and almost up to date. Old people are still frightened; young men and women still gather on Simchat Torah to sing their allegiance to Jewish memory. They still urge the visitor to remember them.

Russian Jews still want to remain Jews. Vladimir Slepak, Ida Nudel, Victor Brailovsky, Iosif Begun are known everywhere for

*Persons denied permission to emigrate.—*ed.*

their courage, but others who are less known are no less courageous. Thousands and thousands of active or potential Refuseniks
are ready to become official outcasts while waiting for exit permits. And, while waiting, they must rely on miracles or on Jewish
solidarity for their daily sustenance. They are dismissed from
their positions, they are abandoned by their colleagues, and,
more often than not, they are harassed by the police. And yet,
more and more Jews express their eagerness to leave for places
where they can live their lives as Jews.

During my third visit to Moscow in 1973, I spent a long, unfor-
gettable night with forty to fifty leaders of Refusenik groups. What
they told me then will remain with me. They spoke of their hope,
of their faith, of their obstinate stubbornness to cling to that faith,
to share that hope.

Some of them have been waiting five, six, seven years for au-
thorizations; still, they are not discouraged. "If necessary, I shall
wait another five years," said one woman, a former professor of literature at Moscow University. I asked them whether they needed
anything from New York or Paris. "Yes," they all exclaimed, "send
us books. Only books." I did not need to ask what kind of books. I
knew the answer: Jewish books about Jewish history, Jewish literature, Jewish philosophy, Jewish life in Israel and in the Diaspora.
Nothing is as rewarding for a visitor as feeling their thirst for learn-
ing. They meet in private homes and study biblical texts, learn Hebrew songs, analyze recent political developments in Jerusalem, re-
view novels or poems by Jewish writers. Separated geographically
from Jewish life, they attach themselves to it spiritually.

I returned to the Great Synagogue for the Sabbath service.
Somehow, many Moscow Jews had been forewarned. They came
in the hundreds. The hall was packed. The service was solemn
and joyous. On this *Shabbat Khazon*—the Sabbath of Consolation—a chapter of Isaiah is read: "Comfort ye, comfort ye my people." I was invited to the *bimah** to read it. Never since my Bar

---

*Elevated platform in the synagogue from which the Torah is read and sermons are de-
livered.—*ed.*

Mitzvah have I been so moved. I had received permission to address the congregation from the pulpit; never has a speaker had a better audience. The week before, I had visited Warsaw and Auschwitz. I told the congregation: "If Warsaw meant despair, you mean consolation. If we thought of consoling you, we were wrong. You have become a source of consolation for us, Jews in America. In spite of upheavals and oppressions you have chosen to remain Jewish. Is there, can there be a greater reward for your brothers in distant lands?"

An old man looked at me and smiled; a glimmer of recognition lit up in his wrinkled face: "I remember you," he said as he embraced me. "You have not forgotten us." My son, who was then seven, had accompanied me to the synagogue. He was even more welcome than his father. Moscow Jews could not stop admiring him, caressing his hair and kissing his hands, longingly, as though he were a prince from a faraway kingdom. It had been years since they had seen a little Jewish boy saying his prayers in their synagogue. They want to see, they need to meet Jewish children who, for them, represent Jewish endurance and Jewish continuity. But isn't that what they, the Jews of Russia, represent for us? In this respect I became persuaded once more that they have done more for us than we have done for them. We owe them more than they owe us. We are now linked to the same destiny and bound by the same promise.

Just as their freedom depends on ours, our freedom depends on theirs. As long as they cannot fulfill themselves as free Jews, our Jewishness is mutilated and diminished. To remember them is to be remembered by them. To forget what they are is to forget what we are.

In other words: the triumph of Russian Jewry is the triumph of Jewish memory.

ELIE WIESEL

August 1986

TO THE READER

The pages that follow are the report of a witness. Nothing more and nothing else. Their purpose is to draw attention to a problem about which no one should remain unaware. However, they pose only the rudiments of a question, and reflect an anguish; they do not pretend to a solution or remedy.

Having never been involved in political action, I hope that what I have written here will neither exacerbate the cold war nor be used for political purposes. I have never engaged in propaganda, and have no intention of beginning now.

In the course of a trip to the Soviet Union that coincided with the Jewish High Holy Days of 1965, I tried to assess and, if possible, to penetrate the silence of the more than three million Soviet Jews who have, since the Revolution of 1917, lived apart from their people. Regarding other aspects of life in Russia, I do not feel qualified to pass judgment.

Clearly then I must emphasize that I have not attempted to create either a work of literature or an authoritative political analysis. I wish only to add some impressions to the dossier. In doing so, I act as a witness, and my responsibilities are limited to those of a witness.

I went to Russia drawn by the silence of its Jews. I brought back their cry.

ELIE WIESEL

June 1966

The Jews of Silence

I

INTRODUCTION

Their eyes—I must tell you about their eyes. I must begin with that, for their eyes precede all else, and everything is comprehended within them. The rest can wait. It will only confirm what you already know. But their eyes—their eyes flame with a kind of irreducible truth, which burns and is not consumed. Shamed into silence before them, you can only bow your head and accept the judgment. Your only wish now is to see the world as they do. A grown man, a man of wisdom and experience, you are suddenly impotent and terribly impoverished. Those eyes remind you of your childhood, your orphan state, cause you to lose all faith in the power of language. Those eyes negate the value of words; they dispose of the need for speech.

Since my return I have often been asked what I saw in the Soviet Union, what it was I found there. My answer is always the same: eyes. Only eyes, nothing else. Kolkhozi,* steel works, museums, theaters . . . nothing. Only eyes. Is that all? That is enough. I visited many cities, was shown what a tourist is shown, and have forgotten it all. But still the eyes which I cannot forget pursue me; there is no escaping them. Everything I have I would give them, as ransom for my soul.

*Singular, kolkhoz: Soviet collective farm.—*tr.*

I saw thousands, tens of thousands of eyes: in streets and hotels, subways, concert halls, in synagogues—especially in synagogues. Wherever I went they were waiting for me. At times it seemed as though the whole country was filled with nothing but eyes, as if somehow they had assembled there from every corner of the Diaspora, and out of ancient scrolls of agony.

All kinds of eyes, all shades and ages. Wide and narrow, lambent and piercing, somber, harassed. Jewish eyes, reflecting a strange unmediated reality, beyond the bounds of time and farther than the farthest distance. Past or future, nothing eludes them; their gaze seems to apprehend the end of every living generation. God himself must surely possess eyes like these. Like them, He too awaits redemption.

If they could only speak . . . but they do speak. They cry out in a language of their own that compels understanding. What did I learn in Russia? A new language. That is all, and that is enough. It is a language easily learned in a day, at a single meeting, a single visit to a place where Jews assemble, a synagogue. The same eyes accost you in Moscow and Kiev, in Leningrad, Vilna, and Minsk, and in Tbilisi, the capital of the Georgian republic. They all speak the same language, and the story they tell echoes in your mind like a horrible folk tale from days gone by.

For years I refused to believe it. Like many people, I was alive to the reports of Jewish suffering in Russia. I read all the books and articles and heard the testimony given at public meetings or behind closed doors. Yet I was unwilling, or unable, to believe it. I had too many questions, too many doubts and misgivings—not about the fact of Jewish suffering in the Soviet Union but about its scope. I was sure the reports were exaggerated. How else arouse public opinion; how else stir people from their apathy? I relied on my Jewish instinct, telling myself that if the situation were really so black I would of necessity believe it, without demanding proof. My own doubt was sign enough that the reports were exaggerated.

I was mindful, too, of the danger in drawing facile historical analogies between Communist Russia and Europe under the Nazis. Even with regard to the Jewish problem, one is forbidden to make such comparisons. An abyss of blood separates Moscow from Berlin. The distance between them is not only one of geography and ideology; it is the distance between life and death.

If synagogues are being closed in Russia, I reasoned, Jews will simply go on praying in the ones that remain open. Are families prevented from reuniting? A new regime will soon come to power, and policy will change. Does the press conduct a campaign of anti-Semitism? Does it portray Jews as black marketeers, swindlers, drunkards? Does it disparage the State of Israel and malign the Zionist movement? This, too, will pass. Jews are accustomed to living in an unfriendly atmosphere. They have cultivated patience and humor, and they possess to a remarkable degree an understanding of their oppressors. Everything will pass; one must wait. The essential thing is that they be permitted to live, that their existence itself not be endangered, that there be no pogroms. And in Russia there are no pogroms; no one will dispute that. There are no detention camps. The situation, in other words, is not so unbearable.

Of course it could be better. Of course Jews in the free world are obliged to do everything in their power—to move heaven and earth—to see it improved. And of course one must exert pressure on the Kremlin to end discrimination and abolish the economic trials, whose victims were Jews. It is our duty to protest—and I too was among those who protested. But in several instances I was not at all certain whether the charges being leveled against the Soviets were not much too extreme and radical to be true.

I did not believe, for example, that the Russian government had embarked on a clear and relentless policy of "spiritual destruction." Despite, or because of, what had happened in the recent past, I shrank from this idea, which for me will always remain in the exclusive domain of the German people. The Russians had fought against Hitler and in that fight had sacrificed twenty million lives. Of all people, they must know how impossible it is to "destroy" the spirit of a people—of any people. The very thought that they, or anyone, might even be attracted to such an idea struck me as anachronistic and absurd. One must, after all, learn *something* from history.

So I decided to go behind the Iron Curtain to examine the situation with my own eyes. It was no longer possible for me to remain in New York or Tel Aviv and content myself with gestures of solidarity. The problem was too serious for compromises. If the protests were justified, they were in no way strong enough; if not, they had been much too strong. There was no other alternative. One is forbidden to play games with human lives.

In August I made my decision and set the departure date for early in September. I told my travel agent that I meant to spend the High Holy Days and Sukkot* in Russia, and gave him a list of the cities I intended to visit. It was necessary to make advance reservations for hotel rooms and flights between cities, but altogether the technical arrangements took no more than ten days, a minimum of bureaucratic activity. No red tape. Everything went simply and smoothly. The Russian government appears to welcome tourist dollars.

Other preparations proved more difficult. From everything I had read and heard, I knew that this was not to be a normal trip abroad. Over the years I had met more than a few people who had come back shattered by the experience. Something happens to the man whose travels bring him into contact with the Jews of Russia. Whether he goes on business or to see the Bolshoi Ballet, he soon forgets his original purpose and joins the stream. His life changes; the tourist becomes an apostle. And he leaves something of himself behind.

I was aware, then, that something would happen to me, but I did not know what; simply, I depended on its occurrence. I made no plans, I sought no contacts. I refused to arm myself with letters of introduction. I planned to wander about alone, and alone I would meet those I had come to see. I decided not to request personal interviews. I would stay away from official institutions and official spokesmen, visit neither the Foreign Ministry nor the Ministry of Religions. Political manifestoes and worn-out prom-

---

*Feast of Tabernacles (Deuteronomy 16:13–16), an eight-day harvest festival celebrated in early fall.—*tr.*

ises did not interest me. I would not appear at the editorial offices of *Sovietish Heimland.** Whatever Aron Vergelis‡ and his comrades were prepared to tell me they had already repeated countless times before to visitors from the United States, France, and Israel. Nor did I intend to interview the rabbis or lay leaders of the various communities. Why place them in a difficult position? Why confuse them? I could observe their actions from afar.

I would approach Jews who held no position in society, who had never been placed in the Soviet show window by Soviet authorities. I was interested only in them and in what they had to say. They alone, in their anonymity, could describe the conditions under which they live; they alone could tell whether the reports I had heard were true or false—and whether their children and their grandchildren, despite everything, still wish to remain Jews. From them I would learn what we must do to help . . . or if they want our help at all. They alone, I told myself, have the right to speak, to advise, to demand. Theirs is the only voice to which one is obliged to listen. My journey to Russia would be a journey to find them.

I met one of them on my first evening in Moscow, a few hours after my arrival from New York and Paris. Actually, it was he who found me, standing on the sidewalk in front of the synagogue. From my clothes he could tell I was foreign, and he asked me if I spoke Yiddish. The darkness concealed his face. To this day I have no idea whether the first Jew who happened across my path on Russian soil was a young rebel, impelled by stubborn bravado and a Jewish conscience to risk serving as a public spokesman, or an old man glutted with fear who had finally decided, no matter what the consequences, to break his silence. I do not even know whether he was addressing himself to me alone or through me to someone strange, abstract, and distant, who lived as a free man in a land drenched with sunlight and sea.

---

*"Soviet Homeland; a Yiddish magazine established in 1961, now a monthly.—*tr.*
‡Editor of *Sovietish Heimland.*—*tr.*

Why did he refuse to show his face? Perhaps he had none. Perhaps he had left it behind him somewhere in Siberia or, his crime unremembered, in the interrogation cell of a nameless prison. Perhaps he had given it away as a present to his enemies or to God. "Here, take it, I no longer need it. I have another, and it numbers three million."

Perhaps that was the reason he approached me stealthily and in shadow, while all around us thousands of shadows like his stood in the street and waited, powerless to say for whom or for what. Anxious lest I reveal him as a man without a face, he came wrapped in darkness, a simple Jew with no name and no particular destiny, a Jew identical to every other Jew in every city throughout that formidable land.

I heard only his voice, choked and fearful, a few tattered sentences whispered quickly in my ear, the simple gray words used by generations of Jews to describe their condition and fate: "Do you know what is happening to us?" He spoke for a few seconds. He wanted me to know. Finally came a request to remember everything and tell it all. "There is no time. We are nearing the end. Impossible to give you details. You must understand. If I am being watched, I will pay for this conversation. Do not forget."

I was excited and confused. It was too quick and unexpected. Yesterday I sat in New York joking with my friends. We laughed aloud. The transition was too sudden.

He continued to speak, alternating accusation with confession, demanding both justice and mercy at once. I wanted to press his hand, to promise him everything. I didn't dare. Maybe they were really watching us. A handshake could be costly. And so, unconsciously, I slipped into the reality of Jewish fear in Russia.

Suddenly he left me in the middle of a sentence, without saying good-by or waiting for my reaction. He disappeared into the living mass that crowded around the entrance to the synagogue.

I was to meet this Jew again, in Moscow and elsewhere. He always gave some sign by which I could recognize his presence. Once he thrust a note into my pocket; once he touched my arm without saying a word. Once I caught a secret wink of his eye.

Each time I saw him he had changed his appearance. In Kiev I thought he was a construction worker, in Leningrad a civil engineer, in Tbilisi a university professor. But it was always he, for his story was the same and his request never varied. Do not forget; tell it all.

I left something of myself in that country, perhaps as a kind of collateral. Perhaps it was my eyes.

II

FEAR

What are they afraid of? I don't know. Perhaps, afraid to ask, neither do they. I wasn't afraid to ask, but I never got an answer. Official government guides abruptly denied the existence of any such phenomenon, and the Western diplomatic observers whom I consulted simply said that the whole matter was an enigma to them. As for Jews, they smiled at me sadly. "You're an outsider. You wouldn't understand."

I cannot say, then, whether their fear is justified, but I know for a fact that it exists, and that its depths are greater than I had imagined possible. In city after city it confronted me like an impenetrable wall; on the other side, peering out of its own interstices, lurked only the final unknown.

Time after time, people with whom I had been talking slipped away without saying good-by or left me in the middle of a sentence. A person who had conversed with me one day denied knowing me the next. Once a technician who had arranged to meet me in the synagogue to give me particulars concerning a brother in Philadelphia never came. In Moscow I met a French Jew who told me he had come to Russia to visit a sister he had not seen since the war. When he arrived at her house in Lvov she refused to let him in. Later she appeared at his hotel and, in the five minutes she allowed herself to stay, begged him to leave the city, to go back to Moscow, or better, to France. "What did I do?" he cried. And I, to calm him, said, "Nothing. Try to understand, can't you? She's afraid." He began to shout. "Of whom? Of what?" I had no answer.

Perhaps there is none. Perhaps, in the absence of all objective correlatives, their dark and irrational fear exists simply as a thing in itself, without reason or purpose, serving no useful function, incapable of a reasoned justification. It exists because it exists, and it is therefore impossible to fight. No argument, no amount of careful rationalization can hope to unravel the nature of this fear, let alone dislodge its presence.

So far as anyone can tell, the years of terror are over. Stalin's maniacal hold on the country is a chapter in past history. During the last ten years something has *happened* in Russia; changes have taken place which cannot be lightly dismissed as the fictitious products of an efficient propaganda machine. The general populace is beginning to enjoy the benefits of society. Tensions have been noticeably alleviated. If you stop a man in the street, he will not hesitate to talk with you. The person in the airplane seat next to yours will join you in conversation, perhaps even tell jokes. From time to time you may meet an English-speaking citizen who will admit that the workers' homeland has yet to become a paradise on earth. Young people twisting in Russian night clubs would put San Franciscans to shame.

It is only the Jews then who live in permanent fear, in this infectious mystery. "Yes," one occasionally acknowledges, "times have changed, and for the better." But no explanation follows that remark.

"You wouldn't understand anyway."

It is true; I do not understand. Why are they so suspicious? Why do they behave like a community of terrorized captives, on the brink of some awful abyss? No one denies that the Jews have benefited from the recent easing of tension. Writers who had been liquidated or proscribed are now undergoing rehabilitation. Tens of thousands of Jews convicted of "Jewish nationalism" and sentenced to prison have been released. It is no longer dangerous to be known as a Yiddish writer; now and again one hears of

whole evenings devoted to Yiddish songs and public readings of
Yiddish works. A Yiddish magazine—never mind the quality of
the writing—appears regularly each month. The legendary figure
of Solomon Mikhoels* has been revived, and today even Ilya
Ehrenburg‡ takes public pride in the fact that certain Jewish writers were among his closest friends.

Why are they afraid? I tried during my stay to ascertain precisely the consequence of boldness, but it was a futile effort. I bad-
gered my hosts with questions. Is someone who speaks with a Jew
from abroad thrown into prison? If you are seen strolling with a
guest from America or Israel, will you be persecuted? One shred of
evidence was all I required, a single example to convince me of the
clear and present danger, of the imminence of some fatal blow. All
my entreaties failed. "Do me a favor," one Jew told me, "don't ask
simple questions." Another said, "If I told you, you wouldn't believe me. And even if you did you wouldn't understand."

I realized suddenly that there was no common language between us, that they persist in thinking in terms of "we" and "you."
No wonder they refuse to speak to strangers; what's the use of talking? No matter what one says, the meaning is lost. Fear has created a language of its own, and only one who lives with it day after day can hope to master the intricacies of its syntax.

I did, however, succeed in discovering the answer to one riddle . . . not *what* they fear, but whom: informers, Jewish agents
of the secret police who attend synagogue to observe the behavior
of their fellow Jews. They have eyes to see, ears to hear, hands to
write. You must always know who stands behind you, as you
know beyond doubt before whom you will be called to render
your accounts.

At first I refused to believe this. The idea of Jews informing on
Jews was too repellent, especially in the House of God. But they
believe it. Any number of times—in Moscow, in Leningrad, and
particularly in Kiev—I was cautioned by a wink or a low whisper,

---

*Leading Yiddish actor and producer, murdered during the Stalin purges of 1949.—*tr.*
‡1891–1967, Soviet Jewish author; one of a handful who survived the Stalin era.—*ed.*

"Watch out for that one; he works for *them*." Their suspicion can reach the pitch of terror. No one trusts anyone. A Jew profoundly immersed in prayer is pointed out as a fake, a government agent, worshiping not the God of Israel but his enemies. "But how do you know that?" I found myself protesting. "Mightn't you be slandering an honest man for no good reason?"

"Are you telling *us* what is right and what is not?" Their gaze moves between grief and derision. "Do you mean to instruct *us* in matters of guilt and innocence?" Wounded and ashamed, one can only keep silent before such outbursts. Whether their suspicions are founded on fact or not is clearly unimportant. They regard them as factual, and their conviction only serves to compound the fear in which they live.

Occasionally I was witness to incidents that would have seemed funny or absurd had they not been so tragic. "Do you see that redhead," someone would whisper in my ear, "sitting in the third row, pretending to pray with all his might? Keep away from him; he's one of theirs." Not an hour later the redhead himself would approach with lowered voice. "The Jew you were talking with before . . . we know him. He works for them."

You cannot understand these Jews and that, more than anything else, is what shocks you so. Holidays and Sabbaths, when you see them standing outside or gathered in the synagogue, they look oppressed and poor; they seem to be walking, bent over, through a world of the dead, their eyes reflecting sad and distant mysteries. You pity them. Somehow you understand their sadness. Their sadness, but not their fear. I found myself trembling as I asked what had happened to create this wall between us, what it was that prevented me from understanding in the slightest degree the reason for their fear. Am I not a Jew like them? Are we not brothers in the same ancient tradition, sharing a common belief in the eternity of Israel? Do we not observe together the commandment bidding us to sanctify our lives? That such a gap should stretch between us seems impossible. Yet, apparently, everything is possible. Fear remains one point of contact that binds us to one another, but we stand on opposing sides of the line, facing each other. All I can do is pray that my pain reaches out to them, as their fear reaches out to touch me.

If, driven by fear, they were to erupt in communal hysteria, I would feel less pain. If they screamed, wept, succumbed to a mass nervous breakdown, I would know how to react, what to do . . . especially what to think. Analogies would come to mind from recent Jewish history or from the period of the Russian pogroms. But there is nothing in the history of the Jewish people to compare with this enclosed and silent fear. Perhaps it follows its own rules, perhaps not. Perhaps it follows no rules whatsoever but instead denies all logic and escapes all human understanding. Such fear, in its absolute power, can descend only upon those suffering from an overwhelming sense of persecution. Shut off from help, its victims are swiftly brought to the edge of despair, where devoid of hope they await the end.

The situation does on rare occasion reach the level of a larger delusion. On Kol Nidrei* night two young Russians hurled a rock through a window of the Moscow synagogue. They may have been drunk, or simply malicious. In any event the incident was quickly over. No one got excited. But the next morning, in a second synagogue, it was rumored that a serious clash had broken out between the Jews and their attackers.

A similar story came to my attention in Tbilisi, where I was approached one night on a side street by two Jews who asked me to tell everyone I saw about the "terrible things" that had occurred a few days before in Kotaisi, a town about four hundred kilometers away. What had happened? Riots, bloodshed. A number of Jews had been injured, a few imprisoned. I looked into the matter; it was all a lie. No one had been injured, no one imprisoned.

Why was I misinformed? One person I asked suggested that the two were informers who meant to mislead me into spreading false reports. Another said they were good men who had simply spoken out of fear, embellishing what they had heard with details of their own imagining. They had acted under the influ-

*Prayer for remission of vows and oaths, chanted on the eve of Yom Kippur.—*tr.*

ence of that mass paranoia which from time to time attacks the Russian Jewish community.

My first encounter with that community and with the fear that pervades it took place on the night I arrived in Russia. It was Yom Kippur* eve, and as I stood in the Great Synagogue of Moscow, I thought I had come to pray in the company of Marannos,‡ Jews who once each year decided to leave their places of hiding and worship their Creator in public. I felt like a stranger, a gentile, among them.

Yet, on the surface at least, I might have been in any prewar synagogue in Europe or America, not in the very heart of the Russian capital, ten minutes away from the golden domes of the Kremlin and from the infamous "Lublianka," headquarters of the secret sevice, its darkened cellars once the final home of many who were tortured and condemned to die simply because they were Jews.

The sanctuary was brightly lit and crowded. Many were wearing white holiday robes and prayer shawls. As usual the number of older people was large, but there were also many of middle age and quite a few between the ages of twenty and thirty. Three generations had come together—grandfather, who still remembered the edicts of the Czar; his son, who had spent years in a labor camp in Siberia; and his grandson . . . but what was he doing here? Someone, a comrade at school or at work, must have reminded him that after all he, too, was a Jew, only a Jew—by force if not by choice.

The old people prayed with all their hearts; the younger generation sat listening in silence. They seemed thoughtful, worried, distracted. But this was only natural; it was Yom Kippur, the

*Day of Atonement, the most solemn day of the Jewish year, culmination of the Ten Days of Repentance begun on New Year's Day, Rosh HaShanah. Jews traditionally observe a twenty-four-hour fast on Yom Kippur.—*tr.*
‡Specifically, Spanish and Portuguese Jews who openly professed Christianity during and after the medieval Inquisition but continued to practice Judaism in private; hence, "secret Jews."—*tr.*

Day of Judgment. Who shall live and who shall die, who shall be banished and who set free, who shall be afflicted, and who shall be at rest. Thoughts like these occupy the mind of every Jew on this night, wherever he may be. But here they are of immediate moment.

The prayers went on in an orderly fashion, with traditional melodies sung by a cantor and choir. The scrolls of the Torah* were removed from the Ark, and as the procession wound around the pulpit the elderly rabbi, Yehudah-Leib Levin, declared in a trembling voice, "*Or zarua la-tzaddik* . . . Light is sown for the righteous, and gladness for the pure in heart." What light? What gladness? The cantor sang Kol Nidrei. Here and there one heard a quiet sigh. A woman sobbed. And as the final blessing was intoned, "Blessed art Thou who hast kept us alive, and hast sustained us, and enabled us to reach this day," a shudder passed through the congregation. Another year.

Suddenly I sensed my neighbors eying me peculiarly. Their look was unfriendly, insulting. They were examining me, trying to tear an imaginary mask from my face and thus reveal the true purpose of my presence among them. I heard whispers, "Does anyone know him?" No one. "Does anyone know where he's from or why he's here?" No one knew. No one could possibly know. I had spoken to no one, had in fact just arrived, almost directly from the airport. Barely seven hours before I had been in Paris.

Their suspicion did not surprise me, although it did trouble me somewhat. I tried to start a conversation; they pretended not to hear. The fact that I had deliberately chosen to sit in the main part of the synagogue instead of in the visitors' section only increased their mistrust. When I spoke, they pretended not to understand Yiddish. Despite the crowding and the close quarters, a kind of distance opened between us.

It was only when I began to pray aloud, in witless desperation, that the barriers fell. The Prince of Prayer had come to my aid.

---

*The Pentateuch, or Five Books of Moses.—*tr.*

They listened closely, then drew nearer; their hearts opened. They crowded around me. The crush was unbearable, but I loved it. And the questions poured out. Are there Jews in America? In Western Europe? Are they well off? Any news from Israel? Can it resist its enemies? All they wanted was to hear me talk. They refused to answer my questions. "Better not ask," said one. Another said the same. "We can't say, we can't talk," said a third. Why not? "Because. It's dangerous." They turned to me with hunted looks. I could never be one of them, because I would never be in their place. The wall of fear had risen to cut us off.

"Don't talk," one said to me. "Just pray. That is enough. How good it is to know there are young Jews in the world who still know how to pray." I felt like an outsider, a sinner. . . .

I forgot the rabbi and the cantor and the choir. Even God receded from my mind. I closed my eyes and raised my voice in prayer. Never in my life have I prayed with such a sense of devotion.

III

A GIFT

"Masters mine, the Holy Presence dwells not among the sad of heart!" The old man was shouting, a strange fire gleaming in his deep eyes. " 'V'samahta b'hagecha!—And thou shalt rejoice in thy festivals!' A command from the Torah, my masters, a commandment we fulfill at its proper time, no matter where we may be. Today is our festival, the festival of Sukkot—let it be so! I demand the holiday air, for the heavens have decreed that today we rejoice. Too difficult, my masters? Let it be seven times difficult, no one will dampen our joy. We alone determine when to rejoice, when to accept our affliction in love and in silence. What, does it require skill to dance when the heart is glad? No, no, I say just because we cannot raise our heads we must make manifest our gladness, we must utter song with all our being! You have heard me, my masters? Have you understood? If there is no joy, let us create it from nothing, and bestow it as a holiday gift upon our Lord!"

I was in a small Sukkah* somewhere in Leningrad. About a hundred hasidim‡ had pushed their way in to hear an old Jew, his

---

*Booth or tabernacle, hung with fruit of the harvest; commemorates years when Jews lived in huts in the wilderness.—tr.
‡Adherents of Hasidism, a form of Orthodox Judaism that stresses enthusiastic piety. When first established by the Baal Shem Tov in the eighteenth century, Hasidism defined itself in opposition to the rigid legalism of much Eastern European orthodoxy.—tr.

face glowing and his heart raging with heat, his aristocratic features giving transient bodily form to the angel of hope. Everything he touched took fire. When you shook his hand, you felt strengthened and purified . . . protected.

I couldn't take my eyes away from him. I had heard that there were hasidim in Russia, but not like him. I watched him in wonder: a Jew who refused absolutely to submit. Such Jews had celebrated the festivals of Israel in the concentration camps of Europe, in the shadow of the ovens.

The old man spoke. "Moshe! I request you, Moshe, sing us a tune."

Moshe was embarrassed. Unlike the old man, who wore a black *kapota*,*Moshe was dressed in a heavy coat. He was evidently a laborer or low-ranking bureaucrat who had somehow managed to take the day off. An observant Jew, he would stay home tomorrow, too, to celebrate the second day of Sukkot. He would come here to pray, to join his companions in song, and to forget. But he would not sing alone. Perhaps his embarrassment was a result of his not wearing a beard or not having a black *kapota* like the old man.

"I want you to sing." This time it came as a command. "I want our guest to tell the Jews of the world that in Leningrad we know how to sing! Did you hear, Moshe? They must know!"

"Yes, but . . ."

"No buts; not today. The rest of the year is for buts. Not on a holiday, Moshe, not in the Sukkah, not in the presence of a guest from across the sea. Let him be the one to say but. Let him go home and report that the Jews of Russia live under such and such conditions, *but* they still know how to sing."

"What shall I sing?" Moshe's voice took on the tone of an obedient child.

"You know. The Yiddish song I love so. But slowly now, don't hurry it. Slow and gentle, so we hear every word, every note. . . ."

---

*Black robe worn by hasidim.—*tr.*

Moshe closed his eyes and began to sing something in Yiddish, an old tune about a young Jewish boy who went to Heder* and did not want to learn Torah. Now he has a new master, a dog named Balak, who speaks a different language and teaches a different law. But then the young man returns to the days of his childhood. Is it too late? No, the *rebbe*‡ still waits for him. The song was a simple one, a song of experience, its symbolism and its moral transparently clear. Moshe sang and the old man wept. "Again," he begged him. Moshe began again, afraid to disobey. And the old man continued to weep. "Again, Moshe, again!" Five times, twelve times. The old man wept in silence, holding his breath, as if hoping the song would change, would achieve by repetition a different ending. Disappointed, his tears flowed down into his beard.

Hoarse with the effort, Moshe's voice became weaker and weaker until his strength left him altogether. He finished the refrain of the last stanza and stopped. No one moved; nobody uttered a sound as a heavy silence crept over the room. It was as if they feared to revive the present. Even the old one seemed to have become calmer, seemed to be dreaming a distant dream, listening perhaps to a new song, or an old one, from a new world or an old. He may even have entered the Temple of Melody, where now he rested, satisfied.

Suddenly he awoke with a start. "What's happened to you all? Silent again? We must not submit, I tell you! I order you to rejoice, I command you to create a disturbance! A tabernacle in the desert, is that what you say? I want to see a tabernacle within a tabernacle! A festival within a festival! Well, masters mine, what do you say? My good friends, what are you waiting for? Shame! We have a guest, do we not? A guest from across the sea, a messenger! Is this our gift to our brothers? No! I tell you, no! A song of gladness for our guest, let him tell of the gladness in our hearts! Do you hear? I tell you . . ."

---

*Jewish elementary school.—*tr.*
‡Yiddish diminutive of Hebrew *rav*, used primarily to designate a hasidic rabbi.—*tr.*

The sentence unfinished, his head fell forward on his chest and he sobbed like a child.

I stayed with them for a few hours, and I admit I envied them. Where did they get their prodigious courage, where did they find, how did they ever preserve, the hidden power of their faith? What great and terrible mystery has prevented their complete disintegration? Certainly the degree to which they have suffered and the nature of their torment far exceed our own experience. We suffered at the hands of the Nazis, but their oppressors are of a different breed entirely, one apparently devoted to a pure and humane ideology. The tortures inflicted upon us were brought to an end somehow, while they remain caught in an unending ring of terror.

Think a minute. Who were the first, the principal victims of the pogroms? They were. The first to be eliminated in the Communist purges of the thirties. And the first to be murdered by the invading Germans. These first, hundreds of thousands of Jews, old men, women, and children, in the Ukraine and White Russia, from Minsk to Kiev, from Lvov to Vilna. Murdered or thrown alive into mass graves, long before the ovens of Auschwitz began to cover heaven and earth with human ashes. And in Stalin's last years, who were the victims of his mad liquidation programs? They were. The first to be victimized, the last to be redeemed.

Years pass, governments change, patterns of life are altered. But for them, only for them, nothing changes. Or almost nothing. Our nightmare, somehow, was buried; not theirs. Somehow we have grown accustomed to living in abundance and freedom, even in luxury, but especially in freedom. And they? They have grown accustomed to their fear.

Still they have not yielded to despair. In spite of everything, they sing, and they think of us, the Jews outside. They are alone in their battle; yet in their attempts to overcome isolation and terror they work not only for themselves, but for us. For our sake they sing, and to us alone they present this gift of their own making.

I sat with them through their holiday "banquet." Bread, fish, and homemade wine. Nobody missed the meat, and we did nicely without other delicacies. I don't know precisely how, but the Jews sitting around me in that Sukkah managed in some way to overcome their melancholy. They grew flushed and lively, began to tell jokes; it was as if they had just liberated themselves from the dark threat that pursued them. They began to sing, louder and louder; despite the narrow quarters a few began to dance. "O purify our hearts to serve Thee in truth." They accented *truth*. And for that, too, I envied them.

So as not to insult them, I did my best to participate in their happiness. I drank the wine they offered me, ate the bread they sliced especially for me, joined them in their singing. But I was unable to rid myself of the depression that had overcome my spirit. As if in a dream I asked myself over and over, "Why them and not me?" No answer. I knew that tomorrow I would be leaving and they would stay. I promised myself not to forget them—at any rate, not quickly—but I knew already that no matter how I told their story or how much I might try to help them, I could never fulfill my obligation.

"You will tell the Jews outside that you saw us dancing?" The old man's face radiated pride, or perhaps an excess of pain.

"I will tell them."

"And that you heard us singing?"

"I will."

"And were a witness to our rejoicing? You will tell them how we fulfilled the commandment of joy?"

"I will tell them, yes."

Except, I am not sure we deserve their gift, or their joy. Or this story.

They did not complain, they didn't criticize the regime or lament the hard conditions of their lives. It was from other sources that I learned of that, and of the attempts being made to annihilate the Jewish soul by eradicating all memory of its historical identity. Of all this I was informed in other circles, where I learned too that contrary to well-placed rumor, Gedaliah Pechar-

sky* was still in prison, that Leningrad, too, has its share of informers, and that it is impossible to combat the assimilation being
forced on Jewish youth. There is simply no one to teach young
children the Hebrew alphabet. Many are not even circumcised.
The ornate room in the local synagogue which was meant for
wedding ceremonies is rarely used for that purpose anymore.
There are three hundred thousand Jews in Leningrad but less
than ten weddings a year in the synagogue, and no more than five
Bar Mitzvah celebrations. "And the situation here is considered
good. At least," one told me, "I can die as a Jew. In Moscow there
is no longer a Jewish cemetery."

The hasidim do not talk; they only sing. But their song comes
up from a great depth to smash your heart. In their presence you
feel moved to emulate them. Not for their sake, but for your own.

I met them in Moscow, too, and Kiev. They are associated
with various hasidic houses, not just the Lubavitch. And they all
pray in the same synagogue, indeed in the same room, each
group according to its own liturgical formulas. Standing in the
prayer hall you hear the Karlin version with one ear and the
Bratzlaver with the other. Yet their hearts are united in true broth-
erhood. You find no trace of the dissensions that plague most hasidic houses, rather an infinite and uninhibited love of Israel, a
pure solidarity of spirit, and a sanctity which hasidic leaders in Jerusalem or Williamsburg would do well to study.

How many of them are there? No more than a few thousand,
scattered throughout the country, mostly in large cities. Their
children grow up in a Jewish atmosphere and receive a traditional
education. Some of them wear earlocks, and I saw a number of
young men with beards. They gather in a private home to study
Talmud. On Sabbath they attend a lecture on the Bible, and during long winter evenings they tell hasidic wonder tales, passed on
from generation to generation like an underground Oral Law.

*Lay leader of Leningrad Jewish community, arrested and sentenced to prison in 1961 on
charges of espionage.—tr.

What about observance, I asked one of them, certain he would tell me that in light of extenuating circumstances (which one need not go into) it had become necessary to adopt a more lenient attitude toward the commandments. Not at all. On the contrary, he had become stricter than ever in his observance, stricter than Jews elsewhere. His children, for instance, stayed home from school on the Sabbath, although he knew that the consequences were likely to be unpleasant. But there was no alternative, he told me. Perhaps God will take pity; if not, not. His children might suffer, but they will not have desecrated the Sabbath. I quoted him the law: preservation of life supersedes observance of the Sabbath. Not here, he replied. Once we forfeit this commandment, or another like it, the next step is to forfeit all of them. Better not begin in that direction.

How they have managed to live by their sacred tradition, without books, without outside help or encouragement, without the hope of a new generation, is a mystery to me. What supports them? How do they overcome the threat of a petrifying rigidity on the one hand and onrushing assimilation on the other? What hidden forces operate among them? It is all a riddle. The prophet Elijah, the rabbis say, will answer all questions when he comes. But let him come soon, while there are Jews in Russia who still await him, and who will be able to recognize him. If he delays much longer, it may be too late—not only for them, but for us.

IV

BABI YAR

Kiev brings to mind Babi Yar. Kiev *is* Babi Yar. Not that Kiev is not beautiful—it is enchanting. A splendid landscape, parks and palaces, ancient churches and museums, hotels and restaurants, green hills, mountains, and the Dnieper River . . . a tourist's paradise.

But for the Jewish tourist there is only one point of interest in the capital city of the Ukraine, an attraction missing on the map and excluded from guided tours: Babi Yar. Wherever you are taken you cannot escape the feeling that something, the essential thing, is being concealed—the hundreds of thousands of murdered souls who made this metropolis a city of horror. Finally the realization comes that there is really no need for you to be shown that spot, where in the year 1941 between Rosh HaShanah and Yom Kippur who knows how many Jews were buried, dead or alive. The government guides are right; there is no reason to go there, there is nothing to see at Babi Yar. You can see it downtown, in every square and on every street; nothing and everything. All you need is a bit of imagination, and, breaking through the surface, you can then identify Babi Yar with the figure of Bogdan Chmielnitzki,* the man who prefigured it, who prepared the way, the man who made Babi Yar possible.

---

*Cossack chieftain; in 1648 led an insurrection against the Polish and Ukrainian gentry that resulted in the massacre of numerous Jewish communities.—*tr.*

The Ukrainian prides himself on his wars against foreign invaders. Bogdan Chmielnitzki is the national hero of the Ukraine, the same Chmielnitzki who murdered Jews in 1648 and 1649, slaughtering women, children, and old men and destroying defenseless Jewish communities. But this is a small point, it hardly detracts from his heroism. The statues erected in Kiev and elsewhere to perpetuate the memory and example of Chmielnitzki are not intended to commemorate those particular episodes of his life. Did he kill Jews—so what? Hardly a terrible thing, and in any case a thing of the past. Ukrainians are quick to forgive sins of that sort. And if the Jews refuse to forget, that is their business. The Ukrainian sense of reality is more highly developed. Out of esteem for Chmielnitzki they also forget Babi Yar.

As a warrior who hoped to lead his people to independence by the sword, Chmielnitzki failed. But as a murderer of Jews he was successful. The story of Babi Yar will be recorded as his greatest victory.

How many Jews were killed at Babi Yar? Exact estimates are hard to come by. Some say seventy thousand, others a hundred and fifty thousand. Unlike those in Auschwitz, the Germans and their local collaborators here did not bother with statistics . . . perhaps because Ukrainians have no head for figures.

Eyewitnesses say that for months after the killings the ground continued to spurt geysers of blood. One was always treading on corpses. Only recently someone dug up a new mass grave, and it is generally held that this was not the last. So it is impossible to rely on figures; the dead themselves ensure the need for occasional revisions of former estimates.

Non-Jews in Kiev do not like to talk about Babi Yar. Even the quasi-official spokesmen of the Jewish community prefer to pass over it in silence rather than admit the simple, cruel, incriminating fact that the general populace of Kiev, including faithful members of the Communist Party, did not lift a finger to prevent the mass murders. The citizenry saw it all, knew it all and remained silent. No one raised a voice in protest; not a single tear was shed. Stores remained open; life went on as usual. Many of those who lived in Kiev during those days are still there today. Who knows, a few of them might even occupy important municipal positions. Surely it is preferable not to linger over a subject which is far too delicate and far too dangerous to discuss. It is a little like walking over a mine field.

Indeed, those who are prepared to speak the whole truth about Babi Yar can find no one to listen. I was told, for instance, about a woman who rose from her grave in that ravine of death. She had only been wounded. At night she managed to extricate herself from the tangle of bodies that had fallen on top of her and fled, naked. She was given shelter by a Ukrainian. The next day he turned her over to the Germans. Once again she was forced into the long lines, stripped of her clothes, and shot. Once again, she was saved, and this time managed to escape. But her mind had snapped. Now she rants aloud, remembering forgotten things, and people say, "Poor woman, she lives in another world."

A second woman was pointed out to me in the synagogue. She, too, lives in another world, but she was not among those taken out to be shot. She had managed to hide and escape. Her husband, a ritual butcher and a scholar, was caught and killed with the others. After the liberation, his widow somehow received a long letter he had left for her. She shut herself in her room and for three days and three nights read the letter, over and over, hundreds of times, line by line and word by word. Then she went to Babi Yar and called to her husband in a loud voice. The next day she did the same. Now that is all she does, every day of the year, except for Sabbaths and holidays. She doesn't talk to other people, doesn't pay visits to friends or gossip with her neighbors. Whatever she has to say is written in that letter. Everything she has to say she screams out loud at Babi Yar. The dead listen to her. Only the dead.

There is nothing to see, then, at Babi Yar. And whoever goes to see will understand that there is nothing to be seen. Then he will go out of his mind with the shock.

I was in Kiev on the second day of Sukkot. The Jews I found in the synagogue differed from those in other cities. Their fear is more solid, more compact, and perhaps more justified. Their own leaders terrorize them . . . you can feel it in your bones. Nowhere else in Russia did I see such hatred on the part of Jews toward their own leaders.

No sooner had I entered the synagogue—during the occupation it had served as a stable for the German army—when two men appeared at my side to offer me a seat up front in the section reserved for guests. I declined, explaining that I was ready to forego the honor, being neither a rabbi nor a rabbi's son, and that I preferred worshiping together with the common people. The two had not been endowed with a sense of humor. They issued an ultimatum: either I conform to custom and obey their request or go home. They were not in the least reluctant to cause a scene. There had already been a number of cases in which guests were thrown out of the synagogue for being too stubborn. Since I had no choice, I thanked my hosts for their gracious welcome and let them lead me captive to the isolated bench in the front of the hall.

The *gabbai** of the synagogue was a clumsy and vulgar Jew by the name of Jonah Gandelman. His eyes were permanently enraged, his voice continually shouting. He had the domineering character of a military commander and seemed to hold a whip over the congregation. One look from him, and the object of his wrath was cowed into obedience.

What had prompted a man like this, a Jew who had studied Torah in his youth, to seek out this hated role? A lust for power? A need for respect? Or was he perhaps aiming to safeguard the general good, thinking he could help his fellow Jews by standing between them and the outside world?

*Lay leader of Jewish community.—*tr.*

Whatever the reason, he used all the means at his disposal—and they were many and terrible—to separate the worshipers not so much from the government as from the guests who were drawn to the synagogue on Sabbaths and holidays. From where he stood on the pulpit, supervising his flock, he would unabashedly interrupt the service to revile anyone who had dared to give a surreptitious wink in the direction of the visitors' bench.

He did not speak to me. That task had been delegated to his aides who surrounded me on all sides and described to me the state of the Jews in their city. The news was all good. Anti-Semitism in Kiev? God forbid. There were, here and there, a few fanatic Jew haters, but the government was taking proper care of them. What about the poisonous books of Professor Kichko (such as *Judaism without Embellishment*)? Banned from the market. Of course the whole affair was unfortunate, especially since it was a member of the Academy who wrote such lies and the book was printed by a government press and distributed in tens of thousands of copies by an official government agency. It proves that something was rotten, certainly, but what can you do . . . a thing like that can happen anywhere. The important thing is that the book was suppressed, the damage repaired. The Jews have it very good here. They live in absolute freedom, in wealth and abundance. God be praised. Why is there only one synagogue? The Jews are to blame; they have forgotten their religion. And no Jewish school? The youth is at fault; they are not interested in Judaism. And why was the baking of matzah* prohibited for the last couple of years? The ovens were to blame; they didn't conform to health standards. New ones are being built; this year everyone will eat matzah. In general there is no cause for alarm. Whoever wishes to live a Jewish life in Kiev may do so. If you want to eat kosher meat, there are twenty ritual butchers in the neighborhood; take your pick. And *mohalim*?‡ Enough, and more. But the parents are to blame; they want nothing to do with their people. Weddings? Of course, only they are civil ceremo-

---

*Unleavened bread eaten by religious Jews during the holiday of Passover.—*tr.*
‡Singular, *mohel*: ritual circumcisor.—*tr.*

nies; the couples are at fault. Is there a rabbi? Naturally, but he is ill. He is much too old. Is there no one else, will there ever be anyone else to take his place? No. The Jews are at fault.

The Jews sang praises to the God of Israel, the *kohanim** blessed the people of Israel, and the *gabbai's* aides continued to perform their sole function, indicting the children of Israel.

In spite of all this, I established contact with one of the worshipers through a monologue of admonition and bitter testimony. Even as my hosts were doing their best to take my mind off the congregation, I suddenly heard someone chanting an unfamiliar prayer, a prayer not to be found in the Sukkot liturgy. He stood three rows behind me, an elderly man, rather tall, his face suffused with an uncommon purity of expression. He was profoundly immersed in prayer, but mingled in his devotions were snatches of prose intended for my ears alone. "Thou hast chosen us from among all nations . . . don't believe them . . . Thou hast loved us and taken pleasure in us . . . they do not speak for us, they work against us . . . and because of our sins we were exiled from our land . . . know that it is bad for us here, that we are nearing the end . . ."

Thus I received a detailed account of Jewish life in Kiev. Anyone who teaches his children Torah takes a dreadful risk. One who talks to a guest from abroad is reprimanded. They no longer imprison new offenders, but those incarcerated two years ago for the crime of "Jewish nationalism" have yet to be released. Jews are haunted by a relentless insecurity, afraid to speak Yiddish in the street, afraid to approach the government or even their own leaders with religious requests. Anti-Semitism is common among the general populace; Jews are made to suffer from it, but it is forbidden to talk, forbidden to complain. Who knows what the day will bring? The Jewish spirit is deteriorating rapidly; it cannot hold out much longer.

The old Jew prayed on, less to God than to me. All the time he

---

*Members of priestly class, as distinct from "Levites" and "Israelites." Traditionally, descendants of Aaron the High Priest.—*tr.*

seemed to be reading his report out of the prayer book in his hands. It was he, and not the cantor, who served that day as spokesman for the Jewish community, requesting intercession from above.

I spent three full days in Kiev without finding anyone who would take me to Babi Yar. Everyone had an excuse. The Intourist guides were too busy. Jews who had managed to elude my bodyguards and speak with me briefly did not dare to be seen in my company for any length of time. Jonah Gandelman's aides claimed that the question should be taken up with the Office of Tourism, not with them.

Finally I remembered the advice of a Western diplomat I had met in Moscow. I hired a taxi. I gave the driver twenty rubles—a week's salary—and told him, "Babi Yar." He understood immediately and smiled. It was only later that the suspicion arose in my mind that his smile may have been more mocking than friendly.

We traversed the city, passing through the Podol quarter and stopping a moment near the old cemetery. Then we continued for another two kilometers until we reached a broad, open area. In the distance were new housing developments. On my right a new highway, on my left a construction site. "Babi Yar," the driver shrugged his shoulders, as if to explain, *You can see with your own eyes there's nothing here*. He was right. You have to close your eyes to see the thousands falling into an open grave. You have to concentrate with all your energy to hear their cries in this silence which seems so restful and so natural. Where are the mass graves? Where is the blood? Does anything visible remain of that drama of horror? Nothing. Blue skies, a long smooth road, the movement of traffic. And the driver's smile. I stayed there for an hour, my feet glued to the ground, searching for a sign, a memorial of some kind. Nothing. There is nothing to see at Babi Yar.

We returned to the hotel, and I continued on my travels. About a week later I was back in Moscow, where I met with a number of friends in the Western diplomatic corps. One of them told me that the same thing had happened to him. No one would show him Babi Yar, and he, too, wound up hiring a cab. But he was not at all sure that the driver had taken him to the right place; maybe they had gone somewhere else. Presumably that is a common practice in Kiev.

Only then did it occur to me that my driver might have led me astray as well. How could I be sure we had gone to Babi Yar? I remembered his deceitful smile. There was no doubt in my mind now; he had cheated me, had brought me to the wrong spot. My disappointment lasted no more than a minute. Against his wishes the driver had shown me something that I had unconsciously been aware of for some time. Thanks to him and to his deceit, I was finally able to understand that Babi Yar is not a geographical location. Babi Yar is not in Kiev, no. Babi Yar *is* Kiev. It is the entire Ukraine. And that is all one needs to see there.

V

CELEBRATION IN MOSCOW

Where did they all come from? Who sent them here? How did they know it was to be tonight, tonight on Arkhipova Street near the Great Synagogue? Who told them that tens of thousands of boys and girls would gather here to sing and dance and rejoice in the joy of the Torah? They who barely know each other and know even less of Judaism—how did they know that?

I spent hours among them, dazed and excited, agitated by an ancient dream. I forgot the depression that had been building up over the past weeks. I forgot everything except the present and the future. I have seldom felt so proud, so happy, so optimistic. The purest light is born in darkness. Here there is darkness; here there will be light. There must be—it has already begun to burn.

From group to group, from one discussion to the next, from song to song. I walked about, sharing with them a great celebration of victory. I wanted to laugh, to laugh as I have never done before. To hell with the fears of yesterday, to hell with the dread of tomorrow. We have already triumphed.

He who has not witnessed the Rejoicing of the Law in Moscow has never in his life witnessed joy. Had I come to Russia for that alone, it would have been enough.

It had snowed the week before. The day before, it rained. My friends in the diplomatic corps made no attempt to conceal their anxiety. Bad weather would ruin the holiday. Snow—that was all right. But we prayed to Him-who-causeth-the-wind-to-blow-and-the-rain-to-fall to postpone His blessing. For His sake, if not for ours, and for the sake of those who had waited all year long for this night, for this chance to prove that they are mindful of their origins, are mindful of Mount Sinai and their people.

The "festival of youth" has become something of a Russian tradition since it first began four or five years ago during the period of internal easement inaugurated by Nikita Khrushchev. At first the festivals were attended by a few hundred students; then the number grew into the thousands. Now they come in tens of thousands.

Objective observers like to claim that the gatherings have no relation to Jewish religious feeling. Young people come to the synagogue as they would to a club, in order to make new friends and learn new songs and dances. If they had someplace else to go, they wouldn't come to the synagogue.

I should say this explanation is not entirely correct. There is no lack of meeting places in Moscow; young people can get together either downtown, at the university, or at the Komsomol* clubs. If they come to the synagogue, it is because they want to be among Jews and to be at one in their rejoicing with their fellow Jews all over the world, in spite of everything, and precisely because they have received an education of a different sort entirely. They come precisely because of the attempts that have been made to isolate them from their heritage, and they come in defiance of all efforts to make Judaism an object worthy of their hatred.

If they were allowed to live as Jews in a different way, in a different time, or in a different place, it is true that they would probably not gather together at the synagogue on this holiday of light and joy. But they have no alternative, and if they seize the excuse to come to Arkhipova Street, it is a sign that they wish to live as Jews . . . at least once a year, for one full evening. Somehow that will make them capable of waiting until the next time.

But it must not rain. . . .

*Soviet youth movement, attached to the Communist Party.—tr.

I, too, had made preparations for the night of Simchat Torah,* as if for a great test or some meeting with the unknown. I was tense and restless. The many stories I had heard about the celebrations last year and the year before only increased my apprehension. I feared a disappointment. What if they didn't come? Or came, but not in great numbers? Or in great numbers, but not as Jews?

In order not to miss this meeting of three generations, I had arranged to spend the last days of Sukkot in Moscow. Unjustly, I had determined to rely neither on miracles nor on the Soviet airlines. I was afraid my plane might be delayed in Kiev or Leningrad, and I didn't want to arrive in Moscow at the last minute. I could not allow myself to miss this opportunity.

I might have seen the same thing in Leningrad . . . or so I was told. Thousands of students gather at the Leningrad synagogue on the night of Simchat Torah. In Tbilisi, too, young people crowd the synagogue even on an ordinary Sabbath. In Kiev I tried to convince myself that precisely because the Jewish leaders were attempting to suppress Jewish feeling and to drive away the younger generation, it would be worth staying to see what happened. But I was drawn to Moscow. Moscow would be the center; there the climax would occur. What would take place in Moscow could not happen anywhere else, inside Russia or abroad; so I had heard from people who had been there the past three years.

I wanted to see young people, to measure the extent of their Jewishness and discover its means of expression. I rehearsed dozens of questions to ask them, scarcely realizing that when the moment came I would forget them all. While traveling through Russia I had spoken mostly with the elderly or middle-aged. Many of them had expressed anxiety about the younger generation, its increasing estrangement and assimilation. They told me there was little hope for the perpetuation of Judaism in Russia. In America and Europe I had heard Russian representatives, Jewish and non-Jewish, who had taken the line of cold logic—there is no Jewish life

---

*"Rejoicing of the Law"; last day of Sukkot festival, celebrating the completion of weekly Pentateuch readings in the synagogue and the beginning of a new cycle.—*tr.*

in Russia simply because Jewish youth is not interested in it. It is for this reason alone that there are no Yeshivot,* no Jewish grade schools, no Jewish clubs, no writers and no readers and no future. Judaism is strictly for the old. This explanation is put forth by everyone who comes from Moscow to speak about the "Jewish problem" in Russia. Full blame is placed upon the younger generation.

But tonight we would discover the truth. Youth itself would take the witness stand. It was years since I had last prepared for the night of Simchat Torah with such anticipation, such a sense of awe and excitement. I knew something would happen, something vast, a revelation. I was taut and fragile as the string on a violin. One must not force things, my friends cautioned me; you expect too much, you will never be satisfied with anything less than perfection. Patience. As the sun began to set, its rays danced in a fantasy of color over the Kremlin's gilded domes. The sky was clear blue, and there were no clouds. The weather must hold. It must not rain.

It didn't. And it did not snow. There was a cold wind that cut to the bone. That's nothing, my friends said. Young people do not fear the cold. They'll come, if only to warm up.

Apparently the Soviet authorities also expected a large crowd, and they did their best to frighten it away. It had been made known that during the High Holy Days everyone entering the synagogue had been photographed. And now in front of the synagogue two gigantic floodlights had been installed, illuminating the entire street. The Jews were not to forget that someone was watching. The Jews would do well not to become too excited or to betray an overly Jewish character in their rejoicing.

They came nevertheless. Inside, the great hall of the synagogue was crammed with more than two thousand men and women. Many brought their children, for children, too, were to see that the Jews knew how to rejoice. The atmosphere was festive. Young girls stood among the men on the ground floor. The

*Singular, Yeshivah: rabbinic academy, institute for the training of rabbis.—tr.

balcony was overflowing. People smiled at one another. Wherefore was this night different from all other nights? On all other nights we live in fear; tonight we are free men. Tonight one is permitted even to smile at strangers.

The old rabbi seemed calmer than he had on Yom Kippur. The hall buzzed with conversation. Eyes reflected hope and well-being. "Would you give your flag to my grandson?" an elderly man asked an Israeli child who held a pennant in his hand. The boy smiled and nodded. "Here you are." The Russian child took the Jewish flag and kissed it. An informer came up and demanded that the old man return the gift. He hesitated a second, took courage, then said no. His friends stood at his side. The informer bowed his head. Tonight he was alone.

When would the processions begin? They had long since finished the evening prayers. Why were they waiting? It seemed they were just waiting; they had no special reason. They waited because it was pleasant to wait, because it was good to be in the midst of such a large and living crowd, in such a joyful place. If they didn't begin, they wouldn't have to end; they could treasure the perfection of the holiday. Expectation itself became part of the event. They drew it out, trying to expand the holiday past the limits of a single evening or a single day. If one could only remain here, united, until next year.

"Festivities are already under way outside," we were told by new arrivals.

The *gabbai* decided they had to begin. It was already late. One could not stay here all night, or even if one could, it would be dangerous. There was no knowing what people might do or say once they had been given a chance to release their feelings. There was no knowing what the repercussions would be from above.

They had to start. The *gabbai* banged on the table and shouted for silence. Useless. Thousands of whispers grew into an overwhelming roar. The *gabbai* continued shouting, but only those standing nearby, as we were, could hear him. The congregation had come to hear cries of a different sort, or perhaps not to hear anything, just to be present, to partake of the sacred joy of the holiday.

They began. Rabbi Yehudah-Leib Levin was honored with the first verse, "Thou hast caused us to know . . ." He seemed to have recovered his youthful energy. His deep, sorrowful voice seemed more melodious. How many Jews in that hall fully understood his meaning when he sang, "For God is the Lord, there is no other beside Him"?

"The celebrating outside is incredible," we were told.

Inside, too, it was the same. The Israeli ambassador, Mr. Katriel Katz, was given the honor of reciting a verse, "Thy priests shall be clothed in righteousness, and thy faithful ones rejoice." His voice, too, was lost in the roar of whispers, but his title was known, and the enthusiasm mounted. People stood on tiptoe to see the representative of the sovereign State of Israel. His presence made them straighten up; they seemed taller.

The scrolls of the Torah were taken from the Ark and the dignitaries of the community invited to lead the first procession. The night before, I had participated in this ceremony in a small side chamber where the hasidim pray. All the guests had been called for the first procession. Rabbi Levin had also been there, and we danced and danced until our strength gave out. We sang hasidic and Israeli songs in Yiddish and Hebrew. A tall, awkward, red-faced Jew had suddenly broken into the circle and caught the rabbi's arm. "Come, Rabbi, let us fulfill the commandment to dance! We must gladden our hearts for the Torah!" The two of them danced as we clapped our hands in time. The rabbi grew tired, but his partner goaded him on, more, more! They danced not for themselves but for the entire house of Israel. The tall one's happiness was mingled with rage. He could not sing, and he danced without rhythm in little jumps. His eyes shone with unworldly wrath, and I knew that his joy was real, flowing as it did out of an anger long contained. All year one is forbidden to be angry and forbidden to rejoice. Tonight one is permitted to rejoice. He was crying, too. Why, I do not know. Why does a man cry? Because things are good; because things are bad. Here the question is different: why does a man rejoice? Where does he get the strength to rejoice?

But that was last night, and they were hasidim. The people crowding into the synagogue tonight were simple Jews who had come to learn that it was possible to be a Jew and to find reasons for rejoicing . . . or to rejoice for no reason at all. Longbeards and workers, old and young, widows and lovely girls, students and bureaucrats. Among them there were many who had never prayed but who had come to watch the processions and to honor the Torah.

Processions? How could they lead a procession through this mob? The Jews formed an impenetrable living mass. No matter. Here everything was possible. It would take time, but no matter. They had the time, and patience too. Somehow the parade would pass. In the meantime they sang, louder and louder. They were all looking at us, the guests, as if to say, "Well, what's with you? Let's hear something from you." The entire Israeli diplomatic corps was present, together with their wives and children. We sang, "Gather our scattered ones from among the nations, and our dispersed from the corners of the world." Five times, ten times. A number of the diplomats belonged to left-wing parties. In their youth they had scorned religion, and religious people in particular. Tonight they celebrated the holiday with hasidic enthusiasm and abandon. Differences of opinion and class were left behind. An American writer once told me, "As I stood among the Jews of Russia, I became a Jew." He was not alone; many who come here as Israelis also return home as Jews.

"Outside they are turning the world upside down."

Should we go out? There was still time. Here, too, the world was in uproar. Men who had not sung for a year were raising their voices in song. Men who had not seen a Torah all year long were embracing and kissing it with a love bequeathed to them from generations past. Old men lifted their grandchildren onto their shoulders, saying, "Look, and remember." The children looked in wonder and laughed, uncertain what was happening. No matter; they would understand later, and they would remember.

Tzvikah, the vocalist in the Israeli corps, assembled his chorus and gave them the pitch, "David, King of Israel, lives and endures." There was not a Jew in the hall who was not prepared to give his life defending that assertion.

The dignitaries had made their way back to the pulpit. The first procession was over. The *gabbai* announced that all guests were to take part in the second, and the congregation responded with new bursts of song. From one corner came an Israeli tune, "*Heivenu Shalom Aleichem,* We have brought peace unto you"; from another, "*Hava Nagilah,* Come let us rejoice." A third group preferred a traditional song, "Blessed is our God who created us in His honor and separated us from the nations and implanted in us eternal life." Instead of resisting one another, the various songs seemed to fuse into a single melodic affirmation. Those who had spent years in prison or in Siberia, those who had only recently become aware of their Jewishness, now proclaimed their unity: one people, one Torah. Each of them had stood once at the foot of Mount Sinai and heard the word, "*Anochi*—I am the Lord thy God." Each of them had received the promise of eternity.

We held the scrolls tightly to our chests and tried to make our way through the congregation. But instead of opening a path for us they pressed in closer, as if to block the way completely. They wanted us to stay among them. We were surrounded by a sea of faces, creased, joyful, unmasked. Hats of all kinds, skullcaps of every color, handkerchiefs in place of head covering. A young girl clapped her hands, an old man lifted up his eyes as if in prayer, a laborer sighed joyfully. Old men and their children and their children's children—everyone wanted to touch the Torah, to touch us. Everyone had something to whisper in our ears, a blessing or a secret. I have never in my life received so many blessings, never in my life been surrounded by so much good will and love. One pressed my hand, a second patted my arm, a third held my clothing. They would not let us move forward. They seemed to be trying to stop the progress of time. Through us they became freer, came closer to the reality of their dreams. They looked upon us as redeeming and protective angels. The fact that we were different, unafraid, was sufficient to elevate us in their eyes to the stature of saints and wonder workers. When I was young, we used to surround the holy *rebbe* in this fashion, begging him to intercede for us before the heavenly tribunal. But here, they asked for nothing. On the contrary, they brought us their gifts, their love, their blessings. Hundreds of them. Be healthy! Be strong! Be courageous! May we see you in the years to come! May we all live until that day! May you prosper! And may you sing! Do you hear? Just sing! A few went further, giving vent to their innermost feelings, but always in a whisper: I have a brother in Israel, a sister in Jerusalem, an uncle in Haifa. Short notices: brother, sister, grandfather, uncle, grandson. No names. They simply wanted us to know that a part of them was there, in the land of Israel. Others used clichés that in any other context would have produced smiles of condescension or contempt. "The people of Israel lives"; "The eternity of Israel shall not prove false"; "The redeemer shall come to Zion soon in our days." A Jew with a laborer's cap falling over his brow pushed forward and announced that he had something to tell me but no one was to hear. He began to hum in my ear the words of "Hatikvah,"* finished the first stanza, and disappeared, his face alight with victory. A woman pleaded with me, "Say something to my daughter. I brought her so she would see Jews who are not ashamed or afraid." The girl was very beautiful, dark and mysterious, with flashing eyes. She said something in Russian; I answered in Hebrew. Neither of us understood the other; yet somehow we did. Her mother was satisfied; she kissed my hand, murmuring, "Thank you, thank you. Will we ever see you again?" I didn't know what to say. I forgot everything I knew, except those two words: Thank you, thank you. Thank you for the gift of this moment, thank you for being alive, for enduring, for knowing how to rejoice and to hope and to dream. Thank you for being Jews like us. And a thousand and one thanks for finding the strength to thank a Jew like me for being a Jew.

---

*Israel national anthem (The Hope).—*tr.*

Our procession lasted about an hour. Pale and drenched with sweat, we relinquished the Torah scrolls to the next group of marchers and returned to our seats in the visitors' section. I was out of breath and exhausted. I wanted to rest, close my eyes and wait for my strength to return. The third procession had begun. The singing reached me as if from a great distance or from behind a curtain, as in a daydream. I had never imagined that the weight and power of this experience would stun me as it did. If I had come for this alone, it would have been sufficient.

"They're going crazy out there. We must join them."

We went. The remaining processions we would celebrate outside. Luckily there was a side door; we did not have to pass through the congregation. They would never have let us go. Two or three "agents" got up to follow us. Let them. The Prince of the Torah protects those who come to rejoice in His name.

The street was unrecognizable. For a second I thought I had been transported to another world, somewhere in Israel or in Brooklyn. Angels and seraphim were serenading the night; King David played his harp. The city burst with gladness and joy. The evening had just begun.

VI

A NIGHT
OF DANCING

Deliberately or not, they had been lying to us. With good intentions or bad, they had misinformed us. They wanted us to despair of Jewish youth in Russia, had attempted to persuade us of its increasing alienation from Jewish life. For years they had spread such lies, supporting them with arguments whose logic was hard to refute. After all, we were talking about the third generation after the Revolution. Even if they wished to be Jewish, where would they begin? Even if they wanted to study Torah, who was there to help them? It is only natural that they have forgotten their past; tomorrow they will have nothing to forget. And we listened, were saddened, but concurred. Yes, there was something to that. What can one do? It was the inevitable result of historical materialism. You cannot demand the impossible.

But they surprised us. Soviet Jewish youth has remained Jewish to a degree beyond anything we could possibly have expected.

I do not know where all these young people came from. They didn't tell me, although I asked. Perhaps there is no one answer, but tens of thousands that are all the same. No matter—they came.

Who sent them? Who persuaded them to come running to spend a Jewish holiday in a Jewish atmosphere and in accordance with traditional Jewish custom? Who told them when and where and why? I was unable to discover. Perhaps they knew but preferred not to say in public. Fine. Let them preserve their secret. All that matters is that they have one and that they came.

Still, there is something strange about it. Tens of thousands of youngsters do not suddenly emerge from nowhere at a specified time and place. Someone had to organize and direct them; someone had to make the contacts, maintain the necessary spirit, and inform them of the date and time. Who made all the preparations? Who breathed the spark into a flame? I didn't ask; they wouldn't have answered. Perhaps it is better for me not to know.

They came in droves. From near and far, from downtown and the suburbs, from the university and from the factories, from school dormitories and from the Komsomol club. They came in groups; they came alone. But once here, they became a single body, voicing a song of praise to the Jewish people and its will to live.

How many were there? Ten thousand? Twenty thousand? More. About thirty thousand. The crush was worse than it had been inside the synagogue. They filled the whole street, spilled over into courtyards, dancing and singing, dancing and singing. They seemed to hover in mid air, Chagall-like, floating above the mass of shadows and colors below, above time, climbing a Jacob's ladder that reached to the heavens, if not higher.

Tomorrow they would descend and scatter, disappear into the innermost parts of Moscow, not to be heard from for another year. But they would return and bring more with them. The line will never break; one who has come will always return.

I moved among them like a sleepwalker, stunned by what I saw and heard, half disbelieving my own senses. I had known they would come, but not in such numbers; I had known they would celebrate, but not that their celebration would be so genuine and so deeply Jewish.

They sang and danced, talked among themselves or with strangers. They were borne along on a crest that seemed incapable of breaking. Their faces reflected a special radiance, their eyes the age-old flame that burned in the house of their ancestors—to which they seemed finally to have returned.

I was swept along in the current, passing from one group to another, from one circle to the next, sharing their happiness and absorbing the sound of their voices.

It was after ten. The cold brought tears to one's eyes. But it was easy to warm up; one had only to join in the singing or start talking with someone.

A girl strummed her guitar and sang a Yiddish folk song, "Buy my cigarettes, take pity on a poor orphan." A few steps away, a boy played "*Heivenu Shalom Aleichem*" on the accordion. Farther on, others were dancing the *hora*. Still another group was heatedly debating Judaism and Israel. "I am a Communist!" a young student shouted. I asked him what he was doing here. "I am also a Jew." Suddenly I wanted to go from one to the other, begging their forgiveness for our lack of faith. Our disappointment in Russian Jewish youth is a thing of our own creating. It is they who reassure us, they who teach us not to despair.

Hour after hour I wandered through that street, which had become a rallying point for pilgrims from every corner of the city. It seemed to have lengthened and widened, become a thing of joy and beauty. It seemed to have taken on a new soul and with it the sanctity of a heavenly dream.

A dark-haired and vivacious girl stood in the middle of a circle, leading a chorus of voices in a series of questions and answers.

"Who are we?"

"Jews!"

"What are we?"

"Jews!"

"What shall we remain?"

"Jews!"

They laughed as they chanted their responses. Someone translated the dialogue for me, urged me to join in the laughter and handclapping. It was a splendid joke. The Kremlin was ten minutes away, and the echoes of the Jewish celebration reached to the tomb of Stalin. "It's too crowded here!" a boy cried. "Next year we celebrate in Red Square!" His audience burst into applause.

"Who are we?" asked the dark-haired girl.

"Jews!"

A little later I went up to talk with her. Would she speak to a stranger? She would. Not afraid? No, not tonight. And other nights? Let's stick to tonight. She was a humanities major at the university. She spoke Yiddish, she said, with her grandfather, sometimes with her parents, and occasionally even with friends when they were alone. Was she religious? Far from it; never had been. Her parents had been born after the Revolution, and even they had received an antireligious education. What did she know about the Jewish religion? That it was based on outdated values. And about the Jewish people? That it was made up of capitalists and swindlers. And the State of Israel? That it was aggressive, racist, and imperialist. Where had she learned all this? From textbooks, government pamphlets, and the press. I asked her why she insisted on remaining Jewish. She hesitated, searching for the proper word, then smiled. "What does it matter what they think of us . . . it's what we think that counts." And she added immediately, "I'll tell you why I'm a Jew. Because I like to sing."

The songs they sang were mostly products of the nineteenth century. The most popular was a Yiddish folk song, "Come let us go together, all of us together, and greet the bride and groom." But they had updated the lyrics, substituting for the last phrase, "Come let us greet the Jewish people," or "the people of Israel," or "the God of Israel and His Torah."

One group of students had formed a human pyramid. The young man at the apex was yelling defiantly, "Nothing can help them! We shall overcome them!" His audience roared back, "Hurrah! Hurrah!"

More cheers came from a nearby group that was celebrating the holiday in a manner decidedly Russian, tossing one of their number into the air. Five times, six, seven. Higher, higher. A girl pleaded with them to stop, but they paid no attention. Eight times, nine, ten. Nothing would happen. Nothing did. A carpet of outstretched hands was waiting to catch the hero upon his return from on high. "Hurrah! Hurrah!"

This is how Russian soldiers celebrated their victory over the Germans, and how the Jews celebrate their triumph over despair.

"What does anyone in America or Israel care if my passport is stamped 'Jewish'? It doesn't matter to me, and it doesn't matter to these young people here tonight. So stop protesting about things that don't bother us. We have long since ceased being ashamed of our Jewishness. We can't hide it anyway. Besides, by accepting it we've managed to turn obedience to the law into an act of free choice."

The man I was talking to had served as a captain in the Red Army and had been decorated in Berlin. Like his father before him, he was a sworn Communist. But like all the rest, he suffered on account of his Jewishness. Were he Russian he would have long ago been appointed a full professor at the university. He was still holding an instructorship in foreign languages. One day, he said, he decided that as long as they made him feel like a Jew, he might as well act accordingly. It was the only way to beat them at their own game. "Two years ago I came to the synagogue on the night of Simchat Torah. I wanted to see Jews, and I wanted to be with them. I didn't tell my wife, who isn't Jewish, or my sixteen-year-old son. Why should I burden him with problems? There was time enough for that. I came back last year for the second time. The youngsters were singing and dancing, almost like tonight. I found myself suddenly in the middle of a group of youngsters, and my heart stopped . . . I was standing face to face with my son. He said he'd been coming for the past three years, but hadn't dared to tell me."

"Would you like to see him?" he asked me.

"Yes, very much."

"He's here, somewhere," he said, gesturing at the crowd as if to say, "Look closely, they are all my son."

I talked with dozens of people. Some of them questioned me incessantly about the Jews abroad; others tried to debate with me the issue of diplomatic relations between Israel and Germany; a few almost openly acknowledged that they suffered because they were Jews. But not one of them criticized the state or the Russian authorities. And they all claimed, "They will never succeed. Jewish youth in Russia will not disappoint us."

Anyone who was there that night can attest to the truth of this statement. Young Jews in Russia want to return to Judaism, but without knowing what it is. Without knowing why, they define themselves as Jews. And they believe in the eternity of the Jewish people, without the slightest notion of the meaning of its mission. That is their tragedy.

Ilya Ehrenburg wrote in his memoirs that he would call himself a Jew as long as a single anti-Semite remained on earth. There is no doubt that this way of thinking is an important factor in bringing young people together at the synagogue to rejoice in the Torah. Precisely because it is not easy to be a Jew in Russia, Jewish consciousness will continue to grow. "We are Jews for spite," one student said to me. There is some accuracy in this. For want of better teachers, it is the anti-Semites who are making them Jews.

I said to one of them, "You don't know Hebrew, you never learned Jewish history, you don't fulfill the commandments, and you don't believe in the God of Israel—in what way are you a Jew?"

He answered, "Apparently you live in a country where Jews can afford the luxury of asking questions. Things are different here. It's enough for a Jew to call himself a Jew. It's enough to fulfill one commandment or to celebrate one Jewish day a year. With us, being Jewish is not a matter of words, but of simple endurance, not of definition but of existence. If my son were to ask me one day what a Jew is, I would tell him that a Jew is one who knows when to ask questions and when to give answers . . . and when to do neither."

"Hurrah!" the voices thundered. "David, King of Israel, lives and endures. Hurrah!"

This evening gave me new hope and encouragement. We need not despair. The Jews in Kiev, Leningrad, and Tbilisi who had complained to me about the doubtful future of Russian Jewry were wrong. They were too pessimistic, and apparently did not know their own children or the hidden forces which prompt them, at least once a year, to affirm their sense of community. Everyone has judged this generation guilty of denying its God and of being ashamed of its Jewishness. They are said to despise all mention of Israel. But it is a lie. Their love for Israel exceeds that of young Jews anywhere else in the world.

If, on this night of dancing, gladness finally overcame fear, it was because of them. If song triumphed over silence, it was their triumph. And it was through them only that the dream of freedom and community became reality. I am still waiting to see tens of thousands of Jews singing and dancing in Times Square or the Place de l'Etoile as they danced here, in the heart of Moscow, on the night of Simchat Torah. They danced until midnight without rest, to let the city know that they are Jews.

VII

SOLITUDE

The Jew who came up to me in a dark side street in Leningrad seemed older and wiser than his years. But perhaps he was not wise at all, only naïve; or perhaps the experience of despair had led him to develop an acute sense of irony; or, who knows, perhaps he was wholly insane.

"We prayed together in the synagogue this morning," he said, as if to justify himself. "I was waiting for a chance to talk to you alone."

Five hours had passed since morning prayers. I had not noticed him, although since then he had trailed me to the library, to my hotel, and through a museum exhibit. He hadn't dared come nearer until he was sure that we weren't being followed.

"I am at your service. We can talk now, if you like."

He was wearing a winter coat and was breathing heavily. The walk had tired him. A smile lay frozen on his thin face. His movements were slow. All the world's undefined weariness seemed to have settled in his large eyes.

"I have a number of questions. I would be grateful if you would be kind enough to answer them."

He has a brother in Israel, I thought, or in America, and he wants me to locate him. Dozens of Jews had approached me with similar requests. It is hard to find a Jewish family in Russia that has not been torn from its relatives. Everyone who comes from

abroad turns into a Bureau of Missing Persons. Do you know
Leib Finkelstein in Philadelphia? Sam Rosenberg in New Jersey?
Isaac Stein in Petach Tikvah? You always say yes. Or that you
know someone who knows them. You promise to get in touch.

"You don't understand. I just want to ask questions. I don't
need help . . . only information."

I looked at him again. Maybe he really was unbalanced? I
waited for an explanation, but instead he began a strange monologue, answering his own questions, explaining away his own
doubts. He didn't give me a chance to say a word, but held me
there as a witness to his thoughts. I was simply to listen and to
remember.

"They say there are three million Jews in New York, hah? I
don't believe it. And that in all of America the number comes to
six million, hah? I don't believe it. I hear there are statesmen and
rich industrialists, rabbis and writers and community workers,
and that they're all devoted to their people, dedicated to their
work? I just don't believe it. If it were true, we would know about
it. Don't come to me with fairy tales. The truth is, there are no
Jews in America or anywhere else. Only here."

If he had been in a rage, I would have been less moved by what
he said. But his speech was quiet and restrained devoid of any bit-
terness or complaint. It occurred to me suddenly that I was right
the first time. The man did have a brother in America, more than
one. In his own way he was trying to locate six million lost brothers and exchange with them a sign of life. It was the only way to
overcome his solitude.

In Kiev, on the second day of Sukkot, I left the synagogue after
morning prayers and started toward the Hotel Dnieper, where I
had a room. I sensed that I was being followed. Turning around
suddenly, I saw three Jews standing some distance from me. They
had stopped when I had. I felt sorry for them; they must have
been sent by the *gabbai* to keep an eye on me. I shrugged my
shoulders and continued walking. They followed.

A few minutes later I heard one of them quicken his pace. I

slowed down and waited for him to overtake me. "I have to talk to you," he hissed at me in Yiddish. "It's too dangerous inside. One must beware of informers." I expected him to tell me next that his two friends worked as agents. Similarly grotesque incidents had befallen me in Leningrad and Moscow. I smiled at him. "Aren't you afraid?"

"I've taken precautions. My friends will stay back there to warn me."

He began to describe in gloomy terms the conditions of the 150,000 Jews in Kiev. Nothing new. It was all very general, almost routine by now. The same thing goes on in Minsk and Vilna, in Cracow and Odessa. Only here, there is a long tradition of anti-Semitism, from Chmielnitzki to Babi Yar, providing an added element in the general pattern of terror. The conciliatory enactments of the municipal government have not succeeded in allaying Jewish fears. Legislation and reality are two different and often opposing things. Of the three hundred synagogues and *shtiblach* (prayer rooms) Kiev once had, only one remains open.

He broke off almost in the middle of a sentence and returned to his companions, sending one of them to continue the account. In twenty minutes the third took his turn. Each of them knew what the one before had said; there was no repetition. One spoke about the chief *gabbai* and his cruelty toward the old rabbi; another told about Jews who were still in prison on charges of Zionist-nationalist activity or on suspicion of having committed "economic crimes"; the third stressed the impending doom of Russian Jewry—only a miracle could help.

All three asked the same questions: Why are the Jews outside so silent? Why aren't they doing something? Don't they know what is happening here? Or don't they want to know? Maybe it's easier not to know, to ignore our suffering and carry on with their daily affairs, to act as if we didn't exist.

I could not answer their questions. Why *is* the Jewish world so indifferent to the Jews in Russia? I don't know. I know only that this apathy, from an historical point of view, borders on the criminal. Even if we assume that our protests are useless to change

Kremlin policy, they do change the spiritual climate for the Jew-ish population. They bring Soviet Jews the comforting knowledge of a single fact—that the Jewish people have not forgotten them, that they are not alone.

Justly or unjustly, they think that we have forgotten; they think that we have ignored or abandoned them, that somehow we are all too busy and preoccupied to be interested in their fate. Jewish soli-darity extends to everyone in the world but them. The Jewish state has even begun to help the nations of Asia and Africa, but toward them it displays an attitude of vague and hesitant indifference.

This, more than anything else, is what pains them. They can overcome the rest. After all, they are a people who have never been strangers to persecution and discrimination. They will en-dure, despite the fear which permeates their collective existence. They will submit to neither the pressures nor the seductions of their environment. I repeat that I am not as pessimistic as they are; the youngsters I saw dancing on Simchat Torah convinced me that the end is not yet in sight, the fountain has not yet run dry. But how are they to overcome the pain that springs up from within, their disappointment in us and the desperate conclusions they are inevitably forced to draw about us?

We must realize that the Russian government wants them to feel cut off from world Jewry. The official press censors every news item concerning Jewish action taken on their behalf. It failed to report the march in Washington or the demonstration at Madison Square Garden. The government's purpose is clear: to convince the Russian Jews to abandon their illusory expectations of help from America or Western Europe. They are to depend solely on the good will of the Kremlin, and would, therefore, do well to know their place and to behave accordingly. They may as well forget about the Jewish people abroad, who have betrayed them, or who at the very least regard them as stepchildren.

They do of course receive some news from other sources. They listen to foreign short-wave broadcasts in Russian and Yiddish. The BBC, the Voice of America, and the Voice of Israel provide them with information missing from their local papers. But it is not enough; it is a drop in the ocean. A man needs a strong will to withstand brainwashing.

A number of times I was asked by Russian Jews to detail the various efforts being undertaken abroad in their behalf. I confess that I was ashamed to reveal the truth. I could not bring myself to tell them that only a few thousand Jews went to Washington to take part in the protest march; that the Jews of New York were apparently too busy to fill Madison Square Garden for the demonstration held early in 1965 for the Jews of Russia. I lied to them, exaggerating the figures, telling them that a hundred thousand Jews had assembled on that evening. They looked at me in simple amazement. What? Only a hundred thousand? A hundred thousand out of three million? Is that all?

"Our sense of isolation is a compound of several elements," a professor in a large city told me. "From the Russian point of view we are considered second-class citizens, living on the fringes of society. The new regime has made life easier for everyone but us, or, to be perfectly objective, not in the same way for us. The freedoms it granted to others reached us in truncated form. Nevertheless, this is a form of isolation we can live with. It is the isolation that derives from your relations with us that is so difficult to understand. We feel that we have been expelled by the Jewish people, that we are condemned to live on the borders of Jewish history, that we are not worth the effort of protest. Where we are concerned, there is no point in making sacrifices or in trying to bring about change. You have despaired of us, and you behave as if we didn't exist, as if we were not a part of the Jewish people. See for yourself. The Iron Curtain is gradually being raised . . . it is even beginning to disappear . . . but at the very same time the curtain of solitude is falling more heavily all around us."

A religious Jew told me, "Once upon a time Jews used to declare a day of prayer or a day of fasting to protest the maltreatment of a Jewish community, whether near or far. Tell me, how many such days have you held, and where?"

This is the most powerfully affecting aspect of their plight. I do not like to draw extreme parallels between the condition of the Jews in Russia and that of European Jews during the Holocaust. The analogy is illogical, unfair, and unreal. But from a subjective and emotional point of view it is impossible to escape the impression that the two communities have something in common: a sense of total isolation.

And for this state of affairs it is we, not the Soviet authorities, who will one day be called to judgment. We as well as they are guilty. If we are unable to force Moscow to accept Russian Jews as citizens with equal rights, we can at least make contact with them, so that they may know that their welfare concerns us, that they, too, are our brothers.

Their isolation is so total and so absolute that they will do anything to break out, even for a minute. If they fall upon you, begging for a prayer book, a Jewish calendar, a *talith*,* it is not simply because they are religious; they want something to link them to the rest of their people, something to remind them that somewhere Jewish history continues to be written. Frequently I was approached by young people who wanted anything I could give them, anything at all, so long as it was Jewish. One took the Hebrew newspaper I had in my hand and folded it away in his pocket. For a souvenir, he said, to remind him of the Jews and in the hope that they would remind themselves of him.

The Jews who throng the synagogues do not all come to pray. They come to see Jews, to be in Jewish company, and, if luck is with them, to be near a Jew from abroad. Somewhere in their souls they harbor a dream of unity. Hour after hour they remain in the synagogue. Nowhere else in the world have I seen prayers last so long. On a holiday or even a Sabbath the morning service goes on until one or two in the afternoon. The cantor sings slowly, drawing out every line, every note. No one becomes restless. The congrega-

*Ritual prayer shawl.—*tr.*

tion loves it; the later they go home, the better. In the meantime they spend another hour together, and another, on the one island of comfort they have preserved in a sea of solitude.

The true source of their comfort, however, lies elsewhere, in the knowledge that there are other Jews in the world, whether near or far, who live in freedom, faithful Jews who are not haunted by shadows of fear but proudly evidence their Jewishness for all to see. They crowd around a visitor, questioning him closely about the Jewish communities in America, Western Europe, and, of course, Israel. Young and old, religious or Communist, student or bureaucrat, they prefer to ask rather than answer. Rather than hear your assurances that things will improve for them as well, they want to know whether things will be good or are already good for you, for all those who have been privileged to settle in countries where the word Jew is not a mark of shame. They refuse to talk about themselves; only rarely can you elicit more than a low sigh. They have nothing heretical to say about the regime, and will not criticize government policy. They prefer to listen.

When you tell them that Israel is not on the brink of destruction, that world Jewry is not disintegrating, that Jewish youth in the Diaspora actively identifies with its people, they look satisfied and content. Through you they become aware of themselves as part of a large and vital body. When you tell them that Jews who hold high office in the United States still remain Jews in word and deed, you have justified their faith and made them glad. When they hear of Jewish authors in France who have gained world reputations, of men in Israel who have become legendary figures all over the globe, of American scientists who continue to fulfill the commandments of Judaism, their faces light up with joy and pride.

They have harsh claims to make against world Jewry, but still they pray for its welfare and security. More than once, in Moscow and elsewhere, I was told, "The thought that you are continuing to build a Jewish future in Israel and the West is what helps us to endure. Without that, without you, who knows if we could keep going. . . ."

How much they need to believe in us came home to me in a small and secluded synagogue I had gone to visit during Sukkot. There were about eight hundred Jews there, and I was given the honor of reciting the Haftarah.* They looked at me in silence as I chanted the words of the prophets, but their faces were wet with tears. Why did they weep? It was not in sadness or despair. They wept because they had been made to see that there are still young Jews in the world who can read from the Torah, who have not forgotten the melodies of prayer, who turn to their tradition still as to a fountain of living waters.

Without our knowing it and perhaps without our willing it, we have become their support. Their love for us forges their will to live, although we are always too busy to reply in kind.

The Jew I met on a side street in Leningrad told me that today, the only real Jews live in Russia. Nowhere else. To our eternal shame, he may be right.

*Prophetic lesson read on Sabbaths after weekly portion of Pentateuch.—*tr.*

VIII

THE DREAM OF ISRAEL

If there is one place in the world where the State of Israel is regarded not as a territorial unit operating according to its own laws and within its own borders, but as a distant dream filling the veins of reality with sacred blood, that place is the Soviet Union. It is only the Jews of Russia who have yet to be infected with cynicism toward the Jewish state, who still identify the earthly Jerusalem with its heavenly counterpart, the eternal city that embraces a Temple of Fire.

Isolated behind walls of fear and silence, the Jews of Russia know nothing of the secular affairs of Israel, nothing of the scandals, of the petty political squabbles. They would not believe it anyway. For them the Jewish state is wrapped in a prayer shawl of purest blue. Its citizens are all righteous men and heroes; otherwise, they would not be living there.

It happened on Yom Kippur in the Great Synagogue of Moscow. Outside it was already dark. The last prayer was almost over. Old men wept as the gates of heaven began to close; the Book of Judgment was being sealed—who shall live and who shall die, who shall be set free and who shall be afflicted. Their tears were a last effort to rend the skies and avert some terrible decree.

The hall was tense and crowded; the worshipers perspired heavily, suffocating from the heat and the effects of their day-long fast.

No one complained. Outside, a large crowd was trying to push its way in. There was no room, but somehow they would manage. If there were places for two thousand, there would be places for three. An air of expectancy swept over the congregation.

Something was about to happen. They seemed nervous, serious, as if preparing for a dire and momentous act, a collective act that would be remembered forever.

The cantor finished the last prayer for forgiveness. He quickened his pace, as if rushing toward some critical event. Our Father our King, seal us in the Book of Life. Our Father our King, do it for the sake of the little children. Everyone seemed to be standing on tiptoe. Kaddish.* Another minute. They counted the seconds. The cantor proclaimed, "*Adonai hu haElohim*, God is the Lord!" Seven times, with the congregation responding after him. The old sexton brought the *shofar*.‡ *T'kiah!*** The congregation held its breath. And then it happened. As if in response to a mysterious command from an unknown source, three thousand Jews turned as one body toward the visitors' section, stood up straight and tall, facing the representatives of Israel, looking directly into their eyes, as if trying to read in them their past and their future, the secret of their existence. Then in the awful mounting silence they suddenly burst into a wild spontaneous cry which seemed to issue from a single throat, a single heart: "Next year in Jerusalem! Next year in Jerusalem! Next year in Jerusalem!"

The dramatic intensity of this moment immediately brought to my mind similar occurrences in the Middle Ages, when, with a single nod of the head, with a single declaration of faith, Jews sanctified the Name and died. No one had forced them; of their own free will they had repeated an ancient promise, "We shall do, and we shall listen." Instinctively, without preparation or prior instruction, they had slipped back hundreds of years. Their silence, like their cry, is to be understood not as a prayer, but as an oath of fidelity.

---

*Memorial prayer.—*tr.*
‡Ram's horn, blown during the High Holy Days as a call to repentance.—*tr.*
**Designation for a prolonged blast on the *shofar*.—*tr.*

Some will say: double loyalties. But they will not understand that the loyalty of these Jews does not extend to a foreign power but to a concept and a vision, not to a foreign government but to longings which the act of fidelity itself both defines and symbolizes. For the Jews of Russia, Israel is not simply a geographical location but an abstract messianic principle, a part of their own inner spiritual life. It is perhaps strange that in the homeland of Marxist rationalism there are still Jews who think of Israel as some kind of miracle and speak of it in terms that sound to us like the tritest and most pious of clichés. These Jews have not yet learned to enclose the word Zionism in quotation marks.

There is of course no lack of professional faultfinders. Just read the official press, which portrays Israel as an atavistic, racist, aggressive, and colonialist state, its leaders thorough scoundrels and its citizens exploited and defenseless captives—a kingdom of hell on earth. In one of the larger Russian cities, a government guide told me that a few years ago the Israeli Air Force had attempted to blow up the pyramids . . . in order to ruin the Egyptian tourist industry! He had heard this from "reliable sources." He also knew that in front of the Knesset* building in Jerusalem there was a sign proclaiming that the state will not rest content until it has reconquered Mount Zion, which is situated, he averred, somewhere between Alexandria and Cairo. Similarly, he was prepared to swear on his life that Israel wants war, that it is allied with Nazi criminals in Germany, and that within its borders there is no such thing as individual liberty.

The purpose of such propaganda is to make Israel seem hateful not only to the general populace but to the Jews as well, to undermine the esteem in which they hold the Jewish state, and to convince them finally to relinquish an idea which has failed, a vision of redemption which has somehow been made profane. Jewish readers of Russian newspapers are invited to see for themselves that what takes place in the Jewish state is a violation rather than a fulfillment of their ancestors' millennial dream. Ruled by reac-

*Parliament of Israel.—*tr.*

tionaries, it is a state which persecutes minorities, oppresses the weak, and exploits the poor. How much better then for Russian Jews to turn their backs and blot all memory of Israel from their minds and their hearts.

This form of psychological warfare, directed less against the Jewish state than against the Jewish dream, has thus far failed to achieve its objective. It will continue to fail in the future. The Russian authorities do not understand that the Jews and they are speaking two different languages, are talking about two different things. They fail to understand that it is possible to malign the earthly Jerusalem without injuring in the slightest the Jerusalem which Jews treasure in their dreams as a city innocent of any stain or flaw; their fidelity to that Jerusalem is in essence fidelity to themselves. It is for this reason that they value anything that comes from Israel and honor anyone who comes in its name.

Jews in New York, Paris, or London, even in Tel Aviv, are far more critical of Israel than are most Russian Jews. Somehow, we have all become used to judging Israel by routine secular standards; the hope of yesterday has become today's fact. We have learned to draw clear and distinct lines between dream and reality. But in Russia, Jews have yet to reach this stage of maturity. The simple day-to-day words which produce no reaction in us whatsoever are often capable of reducing them to a state of extreme sentimental emotion. In Moscow I saw a Jew burst into tears when a little girl from Israel said something to him in Hebrew. I sometimes think that if Israel had been established solely for the sake of the Russian Jews, it would have fulfilled its purpose. If it existed solely to demonstrate to them that they must not despair, that a dream is indeed capable of becoming reality, that would have been sufficient.

On the other hand, it may be that our reality exists only, or at least partly, by virtue of their dream.

Were the gates suddenly to open, would all three million Jews in Russia decide to leave and go to Israel? I cannot answer that question. No one can. It is dangerous, and almost impossible, to generalize on this subject.

I did on occasion meet Jews who exclaimed to me, "If only they would load us all on a great cart and send us off to Israel!" But I also talked with young people who said the opposite, "We are not prepared to become immigrants in a new land and begin our lives all over again."

Once, some years ago, during the Stalin era, word came down that Jews would be permitted to register for exit visas. Thousands responded, and they were all imprisoned. Ever since, the Jews have feared a repetition of this incident. Even many of those who have close relatives in Israel, brothers and sisters, hesitate to apply for emigration permits. They prefer to wait . . . and to be silent.

So it is impossible to determine in advance precisely what would happen if and when the hoped for miracle should occur. There are those who believe we will witness a mass movement that will surpass in numbers and enthusiasm all previous emigrations to the land of Israel. Fifty years of Communist rule, they argue, have proved to the Jews that no matter what they do, they will always remain an unwanted element in Russian society, denied the right to live as Jews and yet, as Jews, unable wholly to assimilate into non-Jewish society. Therefore, in the absence of any alternative, young and old alike will take the necessary final step and leave for a country that awaits them with open arms.

Others claim that only the aged will go and perhaps a small percentage of the young. Most young people will draw back at the last moment. They are not prepared to leave for all time the country in which they were born, brought up, and educated, whose language they love, and whose customs they know. The frequency of intermarriage among the young will prove to be another important deterrent. Despite the magical appeal of Israel and despite pressures at home, they will forego the opportunity to emigrate and will remain in Russia.

It is hard to determine which of these two readings is the more plausible. In deciding such questions, one could not rely on the findings of a public opinion poll or questionnaire, even if one dared to undertake such a survey. As in many other areas, we may speak with relative certainty only of subjective impressions.

During my travels I talked with older men, their children, and their grandchildren. I paid a number of visits to their homes and tried to sound them out. On the plane from Moscow to Leningrad I spoke with an electrical engineer; in Kiev I met a factory foreman; in Tbilisi I took a walk with a professor of political science; and in Moscow I spent many hours with students.

From everything they said and did not say, I came to the conclusion that many Russian Jews would seize an opportunity to flee the fear and discrimination which pursue them. To be more precise, the few would draw the many after them. Once it began, once permission was granted and the first gate opened, they would follow in multitudes. It has always been that way in Jewish history. Few have ever chosen to remain behind, alone.

But I should emphasize that if the Jews of Russia leave their homes it will not be because they oppose the regime or because the objective conditions of their lives are unbearable. Many Russian citizens share those same conditions. They will leave only because of the anti-Jewish atmosphere which—no matter who is at fault—pervades their homeland. Were they allowed to live full Jewish lives, were they not coerced into disowning their tradition, it is very likely that many of them would prefer to remain rather than set out for the unknown.

But as a Jew in Kiev said to me, "If only this theoretical question became a real one, then we could do without answers."

There is no doubt, however, that Israel occupies a vital and central place in the consciousness of Russian Jews at all ages and all levels. Jews are interested in news from Israel not simply out of curiosity but out of a profound sense of shared purpose. They feel that what happens there also affects them, that their fate is linked with that of the Jewish state. And if they still dream of a messianic future, it is because there, across the sea, an attempt has already been made to establish a third Temple, a third Jewish Commonwealth. From afar, in thought and silent prayer, they strive to take part in that endeavor.

In virtually every Jewish home everyone listens to the broadcasts of the Voice of Israel. In every city I received the latest news from Israel at the synagogue. Members of the congregation would come up to me and whisper the content of Premier Levi Eshkol's latest speech in Tel Aviv, the words of Golda Meir at an assembly of the United Nations, or the most recent threats of Gamal Abdul Nasser. They importune tourists to tell them more and more about life in Israel. Somehow they still find it hard to believe that a Jewish state exists, with its own ministers and its own police force, its own army and its own heroes. They know it is all true, but it sounds like a dream. Again and again they ask you if the state is really all that strong, if its army is really capable of defeating the enemy, if its scientists are really internationally known, if its presence in Africa is really felt as much as that of the United States or the Soviet Union.

When you tell them what they want to hear, something takes fire in their eyes; they regard you as a messenger from a land of dreams, as the scion of a royal house. The waves of love I felt on the night of Simchat Torah in the Moscow synagogue were another expression of their reverence for the Jewish state and its significance for them. Their tears, their secret handshakes, their whispered messages and cautious touches, their short blessings, all indicated that I was a different kind of Jew from them, a kind they would like to become . . . unafraid, and free to express their feelings about the State of Israel. I shall never forget the Jew who came up to me in the synagogue and almost without moving his lips said under his breath, "I spent ten years in a prison and a labor camp for so-called Jewish nationalist activities; now I know that it was worth it." Or the sociology student who suddenly began to talk to me in broken Hebrew, in phrases that seemed to be taken out of a beginners' textbook, "This is a house. This is a man. This is a window. I am a Jew." That was all he said before he disappeared with a smile into the crowd.

And how can I forget the young people singing in Hebrew?

The girls teaching their boyfriends Yiddish and Israeli songs which they had learned God knows how and God knows where; or the melancholy look of the waitress who saw the Hebrew newspaper in my hand? The hundreds of Jews who in a thousand different ways and through multifarious means always succeeded in identifying themselves to me, with a wink of the eye, a Hebrew word—how can I forget them?

"If something should happen to Israel, we would be totally lost. If that hope also explodes, we will no longer be able to hold out, we will have to submit." This was the opinion of a technician, about forty years old, who was born in Russia, studied in a Russian high school and university, served in the Red Army, and was wounded twice in the service of his homeland.

"If you could emigrate to Israel," I asked him, "would you go?"

He was a Communist. "That's a question I'd rather not think about."

A paradox, perhaps. Can one be loyal to two opposing ideas at the same time? Apparently so. For the Jews of Russia everything is possible. It must be, or they would have given up long ago.

A Communist student tried to argue with me one evening about relations between Israel and Germany. He had prepared all the right questions. "Why have they sold weapons and uniforms to the Bundeswehr? Why did they approve German rearmament? Why have they established diplomatic ties with Bonn?"

To be truthful, I did not feel very comfortable with these questions. I have my own opinions on this subject. But Moscow was not the proper place in which to begin criticizing Israel's German policy. Instead, I answered with another question. "Is it all right for Moscow to do this? Is Moscow permitted to encourage trade relations with Bonn? Or to defend the legitimacy of East Germany? Why did Russia extend such a warm welcome to Alfred Krupp?* And why are there more German tourists in Russia than any other kind?"

---

*German industrialist whose factories produced arms for the Third Reich during World War II.—*tr.*

"That's different," he said finally, in some confusion. "Don't compare Israel to Russia."

He did not understand what he was saying. He did not realize that he, too, applied a different standard to Israel, that his relation to the Jewish state was qualitatively different even from his relation to Russia. He expected Israel to be pure and holy; Israel must not soil her hands.

An ancient proverb says: God bestowed two gifts upon men. To some He gave the gift of wine, and to some the faculty of thirst.

He gave the reality of Israel to us; the dream of Israel he left to the Jews of Russia. We are in need of them, just as they are in need of us. Perhaps more.

IX

WHAT THEY EXPECT FROM US

The holidays were over, and the Jewish spirit had once more gone underground. The three generations who had come together for prayer and song once more went their separate ways. Everyone went home, back to work, back to the university; the side streets with their little synagogues took on their usual abandoned look. Only those above forty would appear for Sabbath services; the very old would come each morning. They would pray together, but the magic of the holidays, the public rejoicing, was gone.

It is hard to summarize one's impressions of a trip that included so many powerful experiences, each of them a turning point in one's own life. It is hard to balance them against one another, to draw a line, add them up, point to the total, and say, "Here is the problem; here is its solution." He who has lived through the experience may laugh or cry, but he cannot define it rationally, cannot be content with a scientific or a literary interpretation, cannot build a theoretical system adequate to explain it. He may, if he has the strength left, voice a wordless scream.

In your first confrontation with the Jews of Russia you are forced to abandon whatever intellectual baggage you may have brought with you. Logic, you suddenly realize, will not help you here. You have your logic, they have theirs, and the distance between the two cannot be bridged by words. The more you see of them the surer you become that everything you have thought or known till now is worthless; here you must begin anew. This strange new world has customs and laws totally unfamiliar to you; language operates on a level you cannot hope to comprehend. You understand nothing they tell you, and when they explain, you believe nothing. You feel as though you have been propelled into a realm of the absurd; when you try to describe it, your description has the air of a harrowing scene from a Kafkaesque novel or nightmare.

But the nightmare is not yours. It's theirs.

My summary, then, must be very personal and very short. The condition of the Jews in the Soviet Union is at once more grievous and more hopeful than I had imagined.

On the one hand, the Russian authorities do everything in their power to prevent Jews from conducting their internal affairs within a recognizable organizational framework, with its own self-esteem, its own culture and folklore, its own scale of values. But on the other hand, they do not make it possible for Jews to acculturate to non-Jewish society, a society that is prepared to accept Ukrainians, Uzbeks, and Tartars . . . but not Jews. The impression has been created that Jews are destined to be alien forever.

The Jewish reaction is natural. Since others try to prevent them from living either as Jews or as non-Jews, they decide, despite and even because of the difficulties involved, to preserve their Jewishness. This is the only way I can explain the mass gatherings of Jews in and around the synagogue on Jewish holidays. Most of them come not to pray, not out of a belief in the God of Israel or in His Torah, but out of a desire to identify with the Jewish people—about whom they know next to nothing.

I asked dozens of them, young and old alike, "Who is a Jew? What is Judaism? What makes you a Jew?" They shrugged their shoulders. The questions do not interest them. There is a time to philosophize, a time to accept the commandments of Judaism as a revelation from Sinai, and a time to ask questions. They are

Jews, and that is that; the rest is unimportant. A Jew is one who feels himself a Jew.

Soviet policy with regard to the Jews is thus doubly strange; its two contradictory stratagems produce the same undesired result. Jews remain Jews.

In the central Russian republic (RSFSR), the authorities are displeased because the Jews have not adapted themselves sufficiently to Russian life; they are not Russian enough. Jews interfere with the process of Russification backed by the Kremlin. Despite the many years of coexistence, there is still considerable distance between Abraham and Ivan.

In the Ukraine, in White Russia, and in Lithuania, the complaint is just the opposite. Jews are much too Russian. The local inhabitants, who have not yet abandoned their particular national heritage, regard Jews as the exemplars of the evils of Russification. They accuse them of being more Russian than Russians.

There are contradictions even in the realm of Jewish life itself. How can the great fear in which Jews live all year long be reconciled with their joyful outbursts on the night of Simchat Torah? How can one explain the appearance of tens of thousands of youngsters at the same time and place when it seems improbable that anyone could have organized them? Or how understand the fact that Jewish Communists come in considerable numbers to the Kol Nidrei prayer, that so many young Jews find themselves returning to Judaism without knowing, without having a chance to know, anything about it? Or the mystical attraction that Israel has for men whose parents themselves were born after the Revolution and brought up according to its principles?

These riddles are hard to solve, for the key is found not in our brains but in our hearts. An intellectual approach can succeed only in clouding the issue still further. In the last analysis, this phenomenon can be understood only in the context of the mystery of Jewish survival from ancient times to the present. Its roots lie deep in the vital emotions of the human heart, which is capable of fear even when there seems to be no logical reason for it. But sooner or later, the heart will be proved right. "We are the only Jews left on earth," I had been told. Only they—because they have yet to give up the dream—only they still look for the coming of the Messiah, despite the unbearable pain that accompanies the birth of redemption. Only they—because they have suffered more than all the rest and are worthier than all the rest of the blessing of peace and salvation. Only they—because they have remained alone.

I never heard them say that their lives in Russia were insecure. No one complained of imminent physical danger. On the contrary, compared to the hardships of the Stalin era, their present situation seems ideal. Today no one executes writers or artists for contributing their talents to Jewish culture; no one imprisons a man for speaking Yiddish on the street; if economic trials are still being held, they are no longer publicized or used to provide anti-Jewish propaganda; if there are still anti-Semites—and there are—their influence is not so strong as to create an atmosphere which might incite pogroms.

Of course, being a Jew in Russia is not the easiest or most pleasant thing in the world. Official spokesmen may deny it all they will, but not a day passed when I did not hear reports of discrimination. For a Jew to progress far enough in his career to replace a non-Jew in a given position is almost unheard of. More than feeling insecure, they feel unwanted. It is as simple as that. From all sides they are made to believe that Russia can get along quite nicely without them; in fact, that Russia without them would be a better place. And the ugly truth is that the authorities do nothing to contradict this impression.

It was in Kiev, of all places—the capital of Jewish fear—that someone dared to voice his emotions to me. "Our government is careful to tell everyone living in America or in Europe or in Israel about the wonderful contributions made by Jews to Russian culture. It stresses the fact that the great scientist Lev Landau is a Jew; that the economist Yevsei Lieberman is a Jew; that the violinist David Oistrakh is a Jew. Why do we never read about this in our papers? They do not want us to take pride in the achievements of these men; so they also 'forget' to report that Jewish officers and soldiers were among those who received the highest decorations and were proclaimed 'Heroes of the Soviet Union' in the struggle against the Germans. The world is allowed to know . . . but we are not. If we were permitted to think of them as Jews, we would one day necessarily begin to think of ourselves as Jews, too, and that cannot be allowed to happen."

What does it matter to the authorities that anti-Semites interpret this policy of silence in their own way, telling Jews that they never fought for the fatherland, never shed their blood for Russia? That all they know is business and black marketeering? That they are parasites on the nation? They say to the Jews, "If you lay in the trenches with us, why don't we know about it? If there are among you some who are known for their excellence in any field, why don't we read about it in the newspapers?"

None of this was news to me. In recent years I had heard and read a great deal about the situation of the Jews in the Soviet Union, and I knew that it was bad. I knew that Jews were in a worse position than others, that despite the progress of de-Stalinization they still enjoyed less freedom than other groups within the population. This is not what I meant when I said the situation was more grievous than I had imagined. I was referring to the Jewish fear that lurks in every pair of eyes, that makes itself felt in every conversation. It is a fear that has penetrated the cells of their bodies; it clings to them like a hateful second skin, black and solid as the night, but not so beautiful. It is the thing that cut me more deeply than anything else in my encounter with the Jews of Russia. And I still do not know whether it is justified or not. Possibly it has remained with them from the days of Stalin, but if so, many of the horrors of that period have yet to be uncovered. The general populace feels practically nothing of this fear; apparently everyone but the Jews has managed to forget those days. The Jews alone remain bound in terror, and who can predict when, or if, they will ever be released?

I have no way of knowing whether all three million Russian Jews are haunted by this fear. I visited five cities, and in them I met only those who came to the synagogue during the High Holy Days and Sukkot, in addition to the young people who came to dance and sing in the street on the night of Simchat Torah. So I cannot truthfully assert that all the Jews in Russia live in terror, just as I cannot say that they all feel a strong attachment to the Jewish tradition. I did not meet them all, and those conversations I did manage to have were not conducted in the manner of a formal interview. For understandable reasons and because of objective difficulties, I was not able to choose my interlocutors or even to assure myself that they formed a reliable cross section of the various branches and communities of the Jewish population as a whole.

During my stay in Russia I saw tens of thousands of Jews, and I spoke to several hundred at least. However, I met almost all of them in the same place and under the same conditions . . . in and around the synagogue. And almost all our conversations were brief and fortuitous, unplanned, carried on through an elaborate system of allusion and insinuation. To be perfectly fair, then, I should note that it is almost entirely on these meetings that my impressions are based. It could be that they do not represent the views of those I failed to meet. It is possible that those who did not cross my path do not want to know about Judaism— theirs or anyone else's—that they are not interested in the State of Israel or their Jewish heritage. Everything is possible, but this is unlikely. If the air is unfriendly in Russia, it is unfriendly to them all. If there is an active system of discrimination, it discriminates against them all. And if one reacts in a certain way, it is hard to see why others would not also.

I should add that I did manage to talk fleetingly with Jews outside the synagogue, in restaurants and airports, hotels and trains. Not one of them had anything to say which contradicted what I had heard from the others. Not one of them failed to express his pain, whether by his silence, or a twisted smile, or through words that managed to hide more than they revealed. Jews who did not look like Jews, Jews who had perhaps concealed their Jewishness for a long time, somehow felt the need to identify themselves to me, another Jew.

Before I left for the Soviet Union I determined that the purpose of my trip was to discover if the Jews of Russia really wanted to be Jews. I never imagined that the answer would be so absolute and clear. I could never have foreseen that I would stand in a synagogue surrounded by men of all ages, not only the old; that I would be present at a public gathering of thirty thousand youngsters on the night of Simchat Torah and that they would be singing in Hebrew and Yiddish. Who would have thought that teenagers would be dancing the *hora* on a Moscow street, shouting "David, King of Israel, lives and endures"? Who could have dreamed that some of them—perhaps many of them—would be studying the Hebrew language, would be passing slips of paper back and forth covered with Hebrew words?

On that night of Simchat Torah I happened to be in the company of a Jew from abroad who prided himself on his antireligious and antinationalist convictions, a cold, dry, unsentimental, liberated Jew. The youngsters were singing, "Come let us go together, all of us together, and greet the Jewish people." Unable to contain himself, he burst into tears. The next day he appeared at the synagogue. "Don't think I've become religious," he said to me. "It's not that. But they have made me a better Jew."

Who knows—perhaps our salvation, too, will come from them.

While in Russia I heard two stories about Soviet Jews which indicated the indomitable strength of their convictions. The first concerned an act of communal heroism, the second an example of individual piety. Both stories came to me, as one says, from highly reliable sources.

In a city somewhere in Georgia, the authorities decided to raze the synagogue and use the site for a new Komsomol club. The Jews were ordered to evacuate the building, which they were told had become too old and dilapidated to be used any longer. Their devotion to the synagogue was such that they offered to raise the necessary funds among themselves to build the club elsewhere, if they could be allowed to keep their building. The offer was refused, and in desperate resolve the Jews decided to resist. The workers who arrived with bulldozers to begin clearing the site found them lying down to block the street that led to the synagogue. Men, women, and children, they absolutely refused to move. The authorities were not eager to start a riot. The workers left; the decision to destroy the synagogue was revoked.

The second incident also took place in Georgia, where Jews were known for their defiant stand even during the "black days" of Stalin.

One morning there was a knock at the door of a man who for some years had secretly and at great risk brought dozens of children into the covenant of Abraham. His wife opened the door, and was confronted by a Russian colonel. "Does Comrade K . . . live here?" Terrified, she answered yes. The officer demanded to speak to her husband. "I have heard that you are a *mohel*; true or not?" The man tried to deny it. "Don't waste your breath." The officer commanded the man to get dressed; his wife packed his personal belongings in a satchel. "Take your 'instruments,' " the colonel ordered.

They got into an army vehicle, and the man was blindfolded. They rode for about half an hour, then got out; the colonel opened a door and removed the blindfold. They were standing in a well-furnished apartment. A woman lay in bed, a crib by her side. "You must circumcise my son," the colonel said. The ceremony took five minutes. The father asked the price, but the *mohel* refused to take money. The colonel would not hear of it. He gave the man twenty-five rubles and two bottles of vodka, blindfolded him again, and drove him home.

I do not know whether similar incidents take place every day, in every city or in every family. Perhaps they do—perhaps not. It is possible that not all Jews want or are prepared to circumcise their sons or to fight for their synagogues. But there are Jews who will under no circumstances let themselves be severed from their people.

That is what I wanted to see, and that is what I saw. It is good for us to know; it is essential that we know, both for them and for ourselves. No matter how often it is repeated, the official claim that, apart from a few old men, the majority of Russian Jews wish to forget their Jewish identity is simply untrue.

One of the last Jews I met in Moscow was a rabbinical scholar. In comparing the present situation to that of the recent past, he quoted to me the commentary given by Rabbi Menachem Mendel of Kotzk to a verse from Exodus, "And the King of Egypt died, and the children of Israel sighed by reason of their bondage." The question was raised: All the time Pharaoh was alive the Jews labored and suffered; why, then, did they sigh at his death? Rabbi Menachem Mendel answered that before Pharaoh died, even to sigh had been forbidden. "Do you understand?" the scholar said. "Today we are permitted to sigh . . . although only when no one is listening."

That the Jews in the free world do not heed this sigh will never be forgiven them. Of that I am sure. For the second time in a single generation, we are committing the error of silence.

One may question whether we have any way of knowing that the Jews of Russia really want us to do anything for them. How do we know that our shouts and protests will not bring them harm? These are very serious questions, and I put them to the Russian Jews themselves. Their answer was always the same: "Cry out, cry out until you have no more strength to cry. You must enlist public opinion, you must turn to those with influence, you must involve your governments—the hour is late."

In Kiev a Jew said to me, "I hope you will not have cause to regret that you have abandoned us." And in Moscow a religious Jew said, "The preservation of human life takes precedence over all six hundred thirteen commandments. Don't you know that?

Don't our cries reach you? Or do they reach you but not move you? If that is so, then we are truly lost, because you live in a world wholly guilty, and your hearts have become foul." In every city I heard dozens of cries like these, almost without variation. I was not to forget, I was to tell it all, I was to warn the Jewish communities of the world that their continued indifference would be accounted a horrible crime in the years to come. I promised I would do it, but I wept before them as I promised. I wept because I knew that nothing would help. Our Jews have other problems on their minds. When you tell them what is expected of them in Russia, they shrug their shoulders. It is exaggerated; or, we can do nothing about it; or, we must not do too much lest we be accused of interfering in the cold war. The Jewish brain has killed the Jewish heart. That is why I wept.

I believe with all my soul that despite the suffering, despite the hardship and the fear, the Jews of Russia will withstand the pressure and emerge victorious. But whether or not we shall ever be worthy of their trust, whether or not we shall overcome the pressures we have ourselves created, I cannot say. I returned from the Soviet Union disheartened and depressed. But what torments me most is not the Jews of silence I met in Russia, but the silence of the Jews I live among today.

X

THE RETURN

(Sukkot, October 1966)

Actually, I should have been disappointed. I had in fact anticipated a certain letdown, and had even prepared myself for it. No holiday can be real unless it has something of the miraculous about it, and by definition a miracle must be a single, unique event. In this case, I had seen it all the year before: the ecstatic prayers of the hasidim on the night of Shemini Atzeret*; the processions in the Great Synagogue on Simchat Torah; the furtive questions put in a whisper to foreign guests; the communal singing; the sudden appearance of thousands of youngsters, demonstrating in public their unshakable solidarity with the Jewish people. Such images— sorrowful and sublime at once—had been indelibly engraved upon my memory from my last visit to Moscow in the fall of 1965. My experience then had been so strong, and so deep, that I feared a mere duplication of it would rob the event of one of its most important dimensions, and myself of a priceless memory. What would happen this year had already happened before. It would no longer be a mystery, or a surprise, but would seem somehow natural and routine. I had already seen everything to be seen, and had said about it everything I was prepared to say. There are some visions which I am convinced we must not behold more than once.

Yet I decided to return. Why, I don't myself know. Perhaps be-

*The festival immediately following the seventh day of Sukkot on which a memorial service and a special prayer for rain is recited.—*ed.*

cause I needed to confirm, for myself, that what I had seen and heard the year before was not in the nature of a momentary dream that had suddenly ignited my imagination. Or perhaps I returned because I felt an inner need to spend this particular holiday with these particular Jews. Something, at any rate, drew me to them—to their songs, to their enthusiasm, to their pride. And once among them, I witnessed a second miracle. Far from being disappointed, far from having to undergo the mere repetition of a previous experience, I found myself caught up in new surprises, and overcome by a new shock of recognition. The report I brought back last year was true—that much has not changed; but now I have come to see that its import is both more valid and more serious than even I had thought at the time. It may even be for this new knowledge that I returned.

I arrived in Moscow on October 5, the sixth day of Sukkot. Upon reaching my hotel I learned that a performance would be given that same evening by one of the Soviet Union's few troupes of Yiddish actors, led by the famous singer Anna Gozik. It is virtually impossible to get tickets to these programs, even though they always consist of the same play: Sholom Aleichem's *Wandering Stars*—the only offering in the troupe's repertoire. People who have seen the performance twenty times return avidly for a twenty-first; the troupe visits Moscow only once a year, and the theater is always packed.

I noticed in the audience a considerable number of young people, who followed the action of the play through the whispered translations of their parents and grandparents. Whenever an actor delivered a line that suggested a double meaning, the audience burst into applause and loud bravos—as for instance when Miss Gozik, portraying Uriel daCosta, declared, "I am a Jew, and a Jew I shall remain!" The significance of such an affirmation for the Jews of the Soviet Union cannot be overestimated. The musical theme of that evening was *"Hava Nagilah"*; at the end, everyone in the audience sang it together with the cast.

During intermission I spoke with some of the youngsters I had spotted in the audience. Although I asked them dutifully why they had bothered coming to a Yiddish performance rather than attending a Russian play or ballet, I knew beforehand what they would answer. In fact, they will go to anything that is Jewish, and are irrepressibly curious about the fragments which still remain of a Jewish culture that was once quite powerful in their country. Should a Yiddish theater be established again in Moscow, there would be no difficulty filling the auditorium. Of that I am sure.

The next day I went to the Great Synagogue on Arkhipova Street. The sanctuary had been redecorated since the last time I was inside; it seemed better lit, more attractive. By contrast, however, the venerable chief rabbi, Yehudah-Leib Levin, appeared to have aged. It was clear from the weariness and grief reflected in his dark eyes that he had not yet recovered from the incident that had occurred in his congregation on Yom Kippur, and about which I had heard the night before. In his sermon on that day he had spoken in passing of the "two million" Jews murdered by the Germans twenty-five years before. A number of those present in the synagogue protested, "Six million, not two!" The unfortunate rabbi was forced to explain that he had been referring only to Jews who were Soviet citizens. Unable—or unwilling—to understand why the rabbi felt constrained to differentiate among Jews, especially dead Jews, the congregation protested again. One supposes that they were justified in their complaint, although it is not for us to judge. The rabbi speaks as he is told to speak, and there is no guarantee that another man would have spoken differently.

The sexton had also changed. He too seemed older, less sprightly than a year ago. Who knows what he had gone through since then? Standing some distance from him was the most notorious of the Moscow "informers," a short hunchbacked man—wearing a green hat—whose features bore ugly testimony to his vocation. I myself saw him strike a Jew who dared to ask me for a prayer shawl and *siddur*. * It is estimated that there are at least twenty informers in the Moscow congregation—a number large enough to ensure the perpetuation of a constant sense of fear and suspicion among the others. It was this sense of fear that had been most strongly impressed upon me in my last visit, and that had haunted me throughout the year.

This time, however, I had come not in order to witness Jewish fear, but to participate in a Jewish festival. The following evening was Simchat Torah, the occasion which tens of thousands of Jewish youngsters have chosen as their annual evening of public celebration. During the previous week, posters had appeared on bulletin boards around the university: "The 'symphony' of Simchat Torah will be performed on the night of October 6, as usual, at the usual time and place." On that night, between thirty and forty thousand young Jews appeared outside the Great Synagogue, where they remained almost until dawn, singing and dancing in hasidic abandon.

By now, this holiday has become something of a tradition in the Soviet Union. The numbers of the participants have steadily increased over the years, and this year—although estimates vary according to the hours at which they were made—there appear to have been close to forty thousand youngsters at the Moscow synagogue. The police closed off the neighboring streets to traffic, and doctors and ambulances were stationed nearby in case of need. They were never called upon. Throughout the entire night of dancing, not a single person was injured; no one fainted, no one needed emergency first-aid. No one became drunk or got out of hand. Not a single person was arrested.

(About two or three years ago, the authorities had in fact tried to discourage similar festivities in Leningrad. The young people were asked to disperse. When they refused, about ten of them were arrested on the spot, but the others simply went on singing as if nothing had happened. Since then, the government has

---

*Prayer book.—*ed.*

taken a more tolerant position: it allows Jewish youth to have its one holiday a year.)

As the first young people began to gather in the street outside the Moscow synagogue, I sat inside, waiting for the religious ceremonies to begin. Despite the unbearable crowding, the sanctuary seemed to exude a distinct air of lighthearted cheer. No one complained about the need to stand for long periods of time, or about the lack of room. Everyone—men, women, and children—waited patiently for the processions to begin. Of the four generations that had gathered together this evening, only the oldest knew what it was to pray. The oldsters still keep the tradition, while their grandchildren clearly have no concept of what the Jewish religion entails. They are interested not so much in the Jewish God as in the Jewish people. Yet they too had pushed their way into the synagogue, to see for themselves what was to transpire in front of the Holy Ark.

This year, too, the ceremonies began only after a considerable delay. The congregation was not in a hurry. Friends shook hands, strangers exchanged smiles of greeting. Men and women mixed freely rather than remaining in their customary separate sections. Tonight, all barriers had fallen. Tonight it was permissible to talk, to laugh, to trust in the future. Even to converse with guests from abroad. Tonight, the hunchbacked informer, his eyes bulging with the rage of thwarted authority, was powerless.

The time came to begin. The foreign guests were invited to participate in the first procession, which was led by the chief rabbi himself. Each of us took a Torah scroll, and we set out together on our circuit of the hall. Within a matter of seconds, we had become separated, each of us surrounded by a sea of heads. The Jews refused to let us move. Kissing the Torah I held in my arms, they showered me with blessings and personal requests: "Tell them in Israel we're with them"; "Be strong, be valiant"; "Don't forget us, we haven't forgotten you." Later I was to find little slips of paper that had been thrust into my pockets: "Next year in Jerusalem"; "Blessings from an old Jew who will die on foreign soil"; a verse from "Hatikvah." One of these pieces of paper had a characteristic request: "Please give me a Hebrew grammar book for my son. He wants to learn. I'll wait for you tonight at ten. Outside." Just like that. No name, no place of meeting.

I tried to move forward, to complete our circuit of the hall; the procession had lasted a long time. Each step forward was like crossing the Red Sea. They refused to let me go. At that moment I had become for them a living link with world Jewry. Here and there I met persons I had spoken with the year before. We managed a few hasty conversations. "Has anything changed?" Nothing. "Is the situation better?" No. "Worse?" No. Three Jews had been sentenced to death for "economic crimes." In one city or another, the sexton of a synagogue had been ordered to sever connections with his co-religionists in Moscow. "Are you still afraid?" Still. "What will happen?" Hope for the best. . . .

On the dais stood a young man wearing glasses; he was an army officer, recently discharged. He held in his arms a Torah scroll which he refused to relinquish. He stood close to the microphone, and his voice rolled out over the hall: "Blessed is our Lord who has created us for His glory . . . O, O, for His glory." The old rabbi began to sing along with him: "Yes, yes . . . for His glory." Hundreds joined in. Only the sexton seemed serious, abstracted—as if he had for the first time discovered the meaning of the words and was quietly taking pity on Him who created such a world for His glory; or perhaps on himself for having been forced to live in such a world.

Last year, the younger people who came to the synagogue had stayed apart from the older Jews. This year, however, they too took part in the festivities, if only as enthusiastic onlookers. Here and there one of them overcame his embarrassment and, following the example of his neighbors, kissed the Torah (even though no one ever told him what is written in it), or sang a hasidic tune he had just learned (without pronouncing the words). A girl clapped her hands, another girl grinned broadly. Behind her stood a boy, preoccupied with his thoughts. I turned to him: "What are *you* doing here?" He answered, "No, you tell me." I knew the answer, even if it had not yet penetrated his own consciousness. He knew that I knew. He smiled at me: he was looking for himself.

This boy's education had failed him. He had been taught to despise his origins—yet he had returned to them. Every attempt had been made to poison his attitude toward Judaism—yet he had retained his ties. Nothing he had learned in school, or in libraries and youth clubs, had succeeded in cutting him off from his community. He had been taught that Judaism was an anachronism, that only criminals frequented the synagogue—yet this too had failed to sway him. He does not, to be sure, come to the synagogue to pray, but he does come to see Jews praying. And that is enough. There are certain silent glances that are worth more than all the prayers composed by the ancients.

As was the case last year, however, the real holiday did not take place inside, but outside in front of the synagogue, where two gigantic floodlights had been installed to illuminate the street. It seemed as if the entire city had emptied its youngsters here, where now they formed into groups, singing and dancing. One circle stood around a girl strumming her guitar and singing Yiddish folk tunes. Farther away, hundreds of students listened to a young man coaxing a melody from his balalaika. There in the corner someone played a harmonica, and there again I found an amateur poet reciting satiric verses about anti-Semitism in Russia. All these voices and melodies seemed to swell together into one pure crescendo of sound, overwhelming the listener and drawing him inexorably into the mounting wave of excitement. Last year the youngsters knew only two or three Yiddish and Hebrew songs. This year they had managed to learn another, and yet another. But their own unique anthem had not changed. It is a song we used to sing at Jewish weddings, when the guests were invited to greet the bride and groom; but the lyrics have been altered by these youngsters so as to refer to their new-found identity: "Come let us go, all of us together, and greet the people Israel."

Walking among them, I suddenly recalled a story of I. L. Peretz about a village boy who played his flute in the synagogue because he didn't know how to pray. Like him, these youngsters also do not know how to pray—nor, perhaps, are they interested in prayer. But they do know how to sing, and how to dance. And as a hasidic *rebbe* once put it, it is also possible to bring the Messiah through the power of dance.

At a certain moment, close to midnight, the lights went out. The two floodlights in front of the synagogue suddenly went dark and stood like blind men. A gloom descended over Arkhipova Street. The crowd stood silent, confused, waiting. Short circuit? No. A subtle hint from above that it was time to break up. One mustn't overdo things. Tomorrow was a schoolday, a workday. It was time to stop, time to go home for another long year. One could return in 1967.

The confusion lasted no more than a minute. It was followed by a groan of disappointment, then a roar of protest. They didn't want to leave. Somebody took a newspaper out of his pocket and set it on fire—the natural act of a man who wished to see where he was. His neighbors quickly followed suit. The idea seemed to please everyone, and word of it was passed along from group to group, from circle to circle. Thousands of newspapers were lit at once, and within a matter of moments the celebration had become transformed into a weird procession of people bearing flaming torches. No one organized this parade, no one arranged for it ahead of time. No one could even have known it would take place. It had happened quite suddenly, and in silence. The quiet was virtually absolute. There was no singing, no talking—only the crackle of burning paper.

Then, in the quiet, about a hundred students climbed onto the balcony of a nearby building. Holding their torches high, they began to chant in unison in both Hebrew and Russian: "The people Israel lives! The people Israel lives! The people Israel lives!" The slogan electrified those standing below, and they roared in answer: "Hurrah! Hurrah! Hurrah!" It was a simple and spontaneous affirmation, but one which should put to rest our doubts about the future of Jewish youth in Russia. There, too, the people Israel lives.

This, perhaps, is the most forceful lesson now to be learned about the Jews of the Soviet Union. Although the same evening had made an overwhelming impression upon me a year ago as well, this time the experience was deeper, and more complete. It had taken on a new and all-important dimension of self-assurance. Not only were more young people present, but they had given a more open and straightforward expression to their Jewishness. It is a mistake to speak of this event as a passing phenomenon; those who are still accustomed to declare at every opportunity that in the course of ten years there will not be a single trace left of Jewish life in Soviet Russia have not seen these youngsters. It is true, of course, that in the past, certain activities took place only in darkness. Young people preferred to meet in the shadows, in side-street courtyards. Unsure of themselves, they could hardly become reconciled to the fact that someone had taken the initiative of setting up special floodlights in the street for the holiday. Despite the general easing of tensions, they remained, justifiably, suspicious. There was no way of knowing whether the man standing off at the side, watching the celebration, was not memorizing names or faces.

This year, however, they had taken the decisive step; they became angry when the lights went out. Now they were demanding both to see and to be seen. For me, their spontaneous torchlight parade is a symbol of their new desire to come up from underground, and to assert their Jewishness in open pride.

On this visit, too, I talked with them for long hours on end. Their knowledge of Jewish matters has not improved. Their faith in Marxism has not been shaken, nor have their ties to Soviet Russia been weakened. I heard not a single word of criticism against the regime in which they live. But I can report that their Jewish consciousness has taken deeper root. Judaism is no longer a matter of apologetics with them. Unlike many of their counterparts in the West, they are not defensive about their Jewishness, but regard it as a basic fact of life which is not open to discussion or philosophical debate.

"Anyone who wants to defame us can go ahead and do so," said a chemistry student I had talked to once before, a year ago. "That's their business. We simply don't answer. We refuse to argue with them. Our answer lies in the fact that we continue to survive—and that we wish to go on surviving."

Another student said, "We refuse to lower ourselves to their level. They've convinced us we're right, and that's the greatest compliment we can pay them."

A girl, a student of Western literature and a friend of them both, said to me in Yiddish: "No one denies that there are anti-Semites here. We present a problem to them, but we've decided not to let them present a problem to us. Once and for all, we've simply refused."

And yet, it is the anti-Semites who have caused these youngsters to return to Judaism, who have coerced them into becoming more Jewish. "It hurts me that our 'revival' has come about because of external, rather than internal, pressures; my only comfort is that this fact hurts the anti-Semites even more," said a man who teaches foreign languages at one of the Soviet universities. A year ago this same man had told me how he had decided not to tell his son about his annual visits to Arkhipova Street, on the night of Simchat Torah, but had then actually met his son here, in the crowd. "This year we came together," he said proudly. I asked him about the rest of the year. Did he talk with his son about Jewish matters? No. His wife is not Jewish, he explained, and there seems no reason to cause trouble at home. "But," he went on, "let's not worry. The situation cannot remain static. It has to change. Once you come to dance on Simchat Torah, you want to live like a Jew the rest of the year too. We'll see."

Indeed, since last year the situation has clearly changed. Young people who formerly knew about the existence of one Jewish holiday have uncovered others. Rosh HaShanah and Yom Kippur do not, it is true, attract them; they want to celebrate, not to fast and grieve. The "festival of freedom" is a far more exciting prospect. On a night during Passover 1966, several hundred youngsters gathered opposite the Moscow synagogue and began to dance and sing. They were the pioneer core, scouting the territory. Had there been no interference, Passover would probably have become another Simchat Torah. Someone, however, suggested to the community leaders that it was inadvisable to overdo such things. The sexton of the synagogue was sent outside to ask them to leave. When this failed, the old rabbi himself came out and begged them to return home. "You're disturbing the peace," he told them. The youngsters finally took pity on these men, and rather than endanger their position with the authorities, decided to leave. They could wait until October. On Simchat Torah all the enthusiasm pent up during the year would finally be released.

About a thousand men and women filled the synagogue on the following day, for the second ceremony of processions. Many had brought presents for the guests: vodka, cake, and apples. They had saved for a week or a month in order to provide this personal gift to the Jews who came to them from afar. A bottle of liquor costs about five rubles—a day's wages for an office worker or skilled laborer. I found myself surrounded by a dozen men, all pleading with me to drink, to accept a piece of cake or an apple. The congregation consists in the main of *pensionnaires*, retired workers. Last night was the youngsters' holiday; today was theirs. "Drink *lehayyim*," a Jew whispered to me. "I've kept this bottle for six months, waiting for this moment." Standing next to him was a man with a red beard, who also urged me to drink: "Drink to us all; who knows, maybe *your* benedictions will be accepted in heaven."

Here and there I heard people say proudly that the whole city was talking about what had happened the night before. Thirty to forty thousand youngsters had taken part in the "symphony of Simchat Torah," and no one had been arrested, or even molested. This morning the chief trustee had contacted the police to ask if everything had been all right. Everything was fine. Not a single incident had been reported—highly unusual in the case of such a large gathering.

The processions ended. Men were being called up to the Torah. We all sang: "Blessed be He who has chosen us from among all nations and given us His Torah." I returned to my bench in the visitors' loge. Hunched in a corner, I read the anonymous notes I had once again found in my pocket: "Next year in Jerusalem"; "Be strong and valiant"; "Don't forget us. . . ."

Suddenly, to my astonishment, I heard singing outside. I thought at first it was the effect of the vodka. But the voices became louder. I left the visitors' section and hurried out to the street. I couldn't believe my eyes. Hundreds of young Jews were there, singing and dancing, exactly like the night before. Where they had come from, how they had managed to leave their classrooms or offices—I don't know. But they had come. Once again the police were called upon to block the street off. Only pedestrians were allowed to pass, and I heard some of them querying the officers about what was going on. One of the policemen replied, "It's just the Jews, celebrating their holiday."

For the second time in twenty-four hours I heard the old familiar songs in Yiddish and Russian. Circles were again formed to dance the *hora*. A young man climbed on the shoulders of his friends, shouting, "Long live the Jewish people!" The crowd roared back its approval, and urged him on. For a minute he seemed at a loss, then recovered himself and began to shout out the names of famous Jewish personalities in the Soviet Union: "Long live Benjamin Dimshitz!" "Long live David Oistrakh!" "Leonid Kogan!" "Yevsei Lieberman!" "Botvinik!" "Maya Plisetskaya!" "Nehama Lipshitz!" All Jews. But the list was quickly exhausted and his audience wanted more. Unthinking, he chose the name of one long forgotten: "Long live Lazar Kaganovitch!" Someone near me asked jokingly whether Kaganovitch was still alive. Yes, he is still alive, but only the Jews remember him. I wonder if it ever crossed his mind that a day would come when his name would be trumpeted aloud outside the synagogue, while he himself was banished from the Kremlin walls.

A boy was pointed out to me who had traveled a distance of thirty miles in order to return a notebook that belonged to a foreign tourist. A second had come all the way from the other end of Moscow because the night before someone had promised to bring him a Hebrew calendar. Others came for no specific reason other than to continue what had been started the night before, as if they had simply resolved to ignore their official allotment of one night a year. It appears that when I expected to see nothing new here this year, I too had not reckoned with Jewish youth.

In all other areas, however, it must be said that the situation remains as petrified as ever. No one holds out any hope that the general discriminatory measures against Jews will be put to an end. German citizens living in the Soviet Union, for instance, have their own schools, their own theater, their own folklore, publishing houses, cultural life, and even radio and television programs. The Jews still have nothing. All others can pride themselves on their national heritage—but not the Jews.

As for the economic trials, it is difficult to ascertain whether they have been completely stopped or not. The press, at any rate, has ceased to publicize them, and that is a good sign. But there are persistent rumors about Jews who have been sentenced to death or imprisonment for alleged economic crimes. These rumors are not spontaneous, nor are they groundless: the place of trial and the names of the accused are known. In addition, the pervasive fear which I encountered a year ago may still be said to exist. This time, too, I came across Jewish tourists from abroad who had tried unsuccessfully to speak with their relatives in Kiev and Minsk. The average Russian citizen does not hesitate to talk with foreigners; Jews shy away from them. In the synagogue I met someone who had been interrogated about a conversation he had had with me last year. They had showed him photographs, had wanted to know every question I asked him and what he had replied. He was released after twenty-four hours, but the effects of the interrogation had yet to wear off. Only because there was a large crowd around us did he feel free to speak with me again. In another place, in different circumstances, he would have avoided me completely. He told me so himself.

On the other hand, I heard of Jews in other cities who had overcome their fear. This year a number of Jews even had the courage to request permission to be reunited with their families abroad. A short while ago, an old hasid was granted an exit visa. Hundreds of his fellow hasidim, singing and dancing, accompanied him to the railway station, to the general astonishment of the other passengers. No one interfered.

Whether or not there will be interference in the future, only time can tell. I believe, however, that no amount of interference will succeed in dampening the new spirit of awakening that breathes in Soviet Jewry, especially among the young. And I believe that the authorities know this. Soviet policy toward the Jews seems to be at a crossroads; the trouble is that no matter which direction it finally takes, the results will in all likelihood be the same. A policy of leniency—even token leniency—will cause many Jews who have hitherto wandered about as strangers among strangers, along the fringes of their people, to return to Judaism. Once it is known that it is permissible to live openly as a Jew—without the fear of public insults and degradation—such people will return in their thousands, for the simple reason that it has been proved to them in their very bones that a Jew cannot live in Russia as a non-Jew.

But an opposite policy—of suppression through the real means of fear and terrorization—will only bring about similar results. The experience of past years has taught us that young Jews will oppose this kind of pressure. They have already demonstrated their unwillingness to surrender either to blandishments or to threats, and their adherence to Judaism will increase precisely as they are asked to reject it. The further they are separated from their people, the more they will assert their identification with it.

It is possible therefore to say that Soviet authorities have missed their opportunity. It may be that at one time—two or three generations ago—it was possible to solve the "Jewish problem" in the Soviet Union, for better or for worse, through a process of voluntary or forced assimilation. Many Jews, if given the opportunity, would perhaps have tried to assimilate and to live as non-Jews; but this was denied them. The general populace refused to accept them as citizens with equal rights. A Jew born a Jew remained a

Jew until the day of his death, whether he liked it or not. His national origin was stamped on all his documents.

By now, however, young Jews in Russia have rejected the solution of assimilation altogether. Although they have had no education in Judaism—except what they have learned from anti-Semitic literature—they cling ferociously to their community. Although nonreligious, they celebrate Jewish holidays and sing Jewish songs. Under no circumstances will they allow their Jewishness to be degraded or killed.

I returned from my second trip to Moscow somewhat encouraged. I am convinced that, however events turn out, these young Jews will continue to seize every available opportunity to demonstrate their solidarity with the Jewish community. I have no doubt that in the not too distant future they will appear in front of the synagogue not just once a year but twice, then three or four times, and then once a month. Something is taking place among Jewish youth in the Soviet Union, and the time has come for us to realize it. Without outside help, without teachers or books, without leaders and meeting places, even without an appropriate spiritual climate, they have managed to survive, and will manage in the future as well. And they will do so, I should add, on their own. They learn Hebrew in secret, translate a Hebrew song into Russian, pass from hand to hand slips of paper with a few lines of Jewish history written on them. They listen to foreign broadcasts and circulate among themselves news of what is happening in world Jewry and in the Jewish state. This activity is not organized by any single person in any single place. Each one of them takes part and feels personally responsible for its success.

Their salvation, then, will come from within themselves, not from us. They may already have realized how futile it is to rely on us—either on our help or on our sympathy—and so have taken their destiny into their own hands. In past years, guests from abroad played an important role on the night of Simchat Torah. Each one of us would be surrounded by hundreds of youngsters, and we would tell them what was happening elsewhere in the world. We taught them new songs. This time, however, we were only observers. A year ago, they seemed to be making a conscious effort to explain and clarify their Jewishness, both for themselves and for others. This year, everything had suddenly become clear. Few of the participants were to be seen engaged in discussions among themselves or with the foreign guests. Rather than besiege us with questions, they appeared content with what they themselves knew. They didn't need us any longer. And the next day, when they came in groups to the synagogue, and began to sing and dance, it was without our knowledge. We went home; they continued to dance and shout: "The people Israel lives!" That song will never die.

XI

EPILOGUE

Things have changed since we last met. Some of your friends are already in their homeland; others are soon to follow. Once opened, the gates will not close again. The Jewish people will not permit it.

Once awakened, Jewish conscience will not drift into slumber again. Nothing will ever be the same as before; either in Russia or outside Russia. We have all changed.

I remember: that night—in autumn 1965—when I first saw you dancing and singing, openly celebrating your faith and that of the people of Israel—the faith in its Torah, that is, in its history. I thought I was dreaming. And if I came back the following year, it was to dream again and take part in your dream, the miraculous dream of young people rejecting exile and the delusions it begets; the astonishing dream of a community forgotten and rediscovered, a community whose bravery and celebrations will be told and retold by those of our legends that speak of the trials and triumphs of Israel.

And do you know what feelings swept over the visitor while he listened to your song? First envy, then pride followed by guilt and humility but also, and that above all, gratitude. Yes, what I felt most strongly was gratitude, for, you see, I belong to a generation

Part of this Epilogue was originally published in 1973 in the *Jewish Chronicle*, London, under the title "Letter to a Young Jew in the U.S.S.R." (trans. Lionel Simmonds).

that has learned to resist dreams, that is afraid of dreams. Today, thanks to you, I can dream again and I am grateful. Grateful that you allowed me to share your dreams, for on that level every dream becomes adventure.

I must confess to you, however, that after our meetings a strange malaise oppressed me. This witness was reproached for having distorted, if not misrepresented, the sense of your message and perhaps also your struggle, in calling you by a title you hardly merited—the Jews of Silence. Believe me when I say that as far as you are concerned this is a misnomer, a misplaced irony. I never implied that you were the Jews of Silence. On the contrary, I let it be understood that *we* were the Jews of Silence, the Jews enjoying security, the Jews of the Western world.

Again and again I said it, explaining myself repeatedly in public—all to no purpose. How many times did I repeat that Russian Jews have learned to overcome their fear, know how to make their silence heard as a means of action; that theirs is a courage of defiance. No one would listen to me or believe what I said.

The account of Simchat Torah in Moscow they described as imaginary. They said to me: "What you have told us is all very nice, too nice to be true." That fifty years after the Revolution there should be young people in Russia who sang in the streets of their desire to express their identity, who proclaimed their desire to link their destiny with the destiny of their people, who secretly learned what was not allowed to be taught them in school—all this was held to be a myth, irrational, a revelation of the impossible.

People refused to believe that it was the whole truth, because it was more convenient to do so. A Jew in fear, that was natural; a Jew stronger than his fear did not exist. They preferred to lavish their pity on the one rather than to evince their admiration for the other. And quite clearly, the one response *you* did not wish for was that of pity, that facile pity reserved for the weak and the desperate.

Desperate, you? Your capacity for hope does not date from today. Feeble, you? You have more strength and it is more stubborn than ours. You proved it to us in Leningrad, in Riga, in Kishinev, and you continue to prove it to us every day.

Now pity was something ingrained in our makeup, in our tradition; not admiration. And since we are confessing, let us add this: we have not done our duty by you. Your fate concerns us, to be sure, but it does not assume a priority for us. Ten years ago, five years ago, there were still Jewish organizations almost everywhere on both sides of the Atlantic which refused to include your struggle on the agenda of their annual conferences.

Their leaders claimed there were more urgent matters to deal with—problems of anti-Semitism, racism, birth control and the war in Vietnam claimed priority. And certainly there was the State of Israel which must receive prior claim.

Sometimes we were told: the interests of Israel demand that we adopt a policy of flexibility, of waiting over the question of Russian Jewry, while we deemed stronger methods to be more appropriate.

In 1967, before the Six Day War, the idea never occurred to anyone even to suggest a different line of action. Israel had absolute priority. There was then a conviction that you yourselves have more than once underlined—that the survival of Israel was vital, more important for you than your immediate security.

Certainly you could have put some embarrassing questions to us. You could have asked us in what way a Jew of Netanya was more important than a Jew of Kiev. But you chose to be our spokesman, and for that you merit our gratitude.

You and you alone had the right at that time to concede Israel priority. By doing so, you established a stronger title than ourselves to be her ally. And from then on the situation lost its last possible trace of ambiguity. All became clear, all became simple. And now we know that for Jews there exists only one destiny. Whatever sustains the Jew of Kiev reassures the Jew of Petach Tikvah; whatever mortifies the old dreamer of Odessa humiliates the young warrior mounting guard over Suez.

Put in another way, we are helping in a new event. For the first time the history of Israel coincides with that of Soviet Judaism and also that of the Diaspora, and inside this history is an interdependence. What happens in Moscow affects the Jew in Haifa, in Baltimore, in Lyon. Your defiance hurled at the Leningrad tribunal merely reflects a greater, wider defiance, essentially meta-physical, which derives from the very essence of our people.

No longer, then, will you hear today calls for prudence and moderation, for we have indeed learned to listen to you. If you tell us it is necessary, above all else, not to keep silent, that it is still necessary to protest, more strongly than ever and more vigor-ously, it is your opinion which will prevail. At the present time we readily admit that you know better than we what we ought to do so that you will not feel alone and abandoned.

You know better than we when we ought to speak and when to keep silent. It's very simple: you are the experts in the matter. I would even say that it is you who will show us the way, not only in that which concerns you but also in that which concerns us. You serve as our exemplar.

Your impact on our existence is a fact of which all of us should take account and you ought to know it, for it will be useful and en-couraging to you to know that each and every one of us feels con-cerned on your behalf. No one is indifferent. Even the students of the New Left or the older faction, even the so-called Progres-sive intellectuals opposed to this or that aspect of Israeli politics, declare their solidarity with you. Clearly that is significant: the sight of you and your deeds, at this moment, is an incontestable attraction. In all the universities it is you who enjoy the limelight, you who are acclaimed. People are more interested in you than in the State of Israel. Why? How can one explain it?

Young people nowadays do not like to explain their motiva-tions. Their elders hardly have the right to explain theirs. Perhaps our young people feel themselves a little guilty toward you. With the traumatic experience of the Holocaust through which they themselves have not lived, they react as a consequence.

In order that their children should not say to them one day: "Where were you when the Jews were fighting for their heritage in Russia? Where were you when our comrades, young Soviet Jews, were thronging the streets outside the synagogue to show themselves and to show others what they were capable of doing?

Where were you during the trials which took place in Leningrad and Riga?"

Perhaps also it is easier for them to identify themselves with you than for their parents to do so. For them you represent the awakening of conscience, the call to adventure and beauty as well as strife in its purest and most humane form.

For your revolt is not accompanied by the shedding of blood or incitement to violence. It is a revolt cleansed of all shame. By affirming your right to your tradition and to your past, you do not deny the right of others. In expressing your desire to rejoin your brethren in their land, you are not seeking to revile or to destroy the ideals of those you seek to leave. The return to your origins has no direct implication that the Revolution has failed, simply that it has not solved what one is accustomed to call the "Jewish question." Your return means that this question cannot be solved internally.

The extent to which the Jew, internally, accomplishes his own destiny can help others to modify theirs. The error of the great Jewish revolutionaries was to think fifty years ago that to realize their universal dream they had first to deny their attachment to Judaism. Now, emanating from this lie, from this denial, whatever it might be, no enduring truth could be proclaimed. At the same time it is possible that the reason for your attraction to young people might be of a more simple order. You surprise them, as you surprised me during my stay among you; and our young people, like their elders, see to their surprise the supreme sacrifice you are prepared to make for our existence—an exceptionally rare phenomenon.

People nowadays are becoming more and more indifferent. Nothing shocks them, nothing astonishes them. They are well on the way to losing their capacity to admire. To them everything seems routine, ordinary, commonplace. The moon walk no longer interests anyone. They no longer know how to worship. They have unlearned the way to earnestness.

This is where you come in. You show us that all is still possible. With less than nothing you restart history. Without school, without teacher, without club, without programs with astronomical budgets, you set yourself up as a Jewish society, mostly underground but existing all over the Soviet Union. And you who know of Jewish existence only through its burdens, suddenly speak of it as a privilege!

And you who ought to be overwhelmed, all you do is sing! You who ought to have all the complexes in the world, seem to have no complex at all and are not prepared to accept any compromise. You who come from so far away teach us fidelity and perhaps truth also.

It's hardly explicable. How have you achieved it? How have you succeeded where so many of our celebrated educators have failed? What have you done to keep going, to manifest such courage before an adversary so powerful and so determined? It certainly borders on the limits of comprehension. The mystics speak of a miracle, others of a mystery, and all over: "We must, we owe it to you, to be worthy of your example." Thus the matter is resolved. The help that our elders refuse you, you offer to our youth. Put in another way, if there is a Jewish revival today, to some extent everywhere, even in the United States, we owe it to you.

Let us be frank: it is to you also that we owe our unity. Without you I doubt that so many Jewish national representative personalities, so many men of state and communal leaders, writers, sociologists, and poets of all shades, would have participated in an act of solidarity with you—with those of you who are in prison, who are in the mental asylums, with those of you who, condemned to forced labor, have been transported to Siberia, and with you who once more are preparing for the festival of Simchat Torah.

We are told that during the Leningrad trial, while the judge was reading out the sentences, the accused shouted: "*Am Yisrael Chai*" (The people Israel lives!). Oh yes, the people Israel do live and will continue to live and you are the proof of that.

The same call stirs us, the same dream, the same force. You see, you have reached the point of no return. We also. You see, there are no longer "Jews of Silence," neither among us in the West nor among you. From Petach Tikvah to Kiev, from Brooklyn to Paris, from Buenos Aires to Oslo it is everywhere the same Jew proclaiming for his brethren the right to speak, the right to sing, the right to dream not in suffering or in punishment but in joy, yes—in joy.

AFTERWORD

By Martin Gilbert

More than twenty years have passed since, during the Jewish High Holy Days of 1965, Elie Wiesel went to the Soviet Union to try, as he then wrote, "to penetrate the silence" of the three million and more Jews who were then living there. He had been drawn by their silence. But, as he explained to his readers, "I brought back their cry."

What a powerful messenger Elie Wiesel turned out to be: the cry that he brought back was not a cry of pain or a cry of fear, but a cry of expectation and a cry of hope. So many books which set out to portray a serious situation succeed only in conveying a negative message, turning the reader against the "victim." Elie Wiesel's book did the reverse: it opened the eyes and roused the sympathies of tens of thousands—indeed hundreds of thousands—of Jews in the Western world to the plight of their fellow Jews cut off from the world Jewish heritage and denied any chance to be reunited with that heritage.

Although the publication of *The Jews of Silence* in 1966 took place at a time when Jews could not leave the Soviet Union for Israel, it gave those Jews a voice they had not had before, certainly not since the far-distant pre-Revolutionary days of Simeon Frug, Chaim Nachman Bialik, and Simon Dubnov.

Elie Wiesel did not merely report that the Jews he met (in Moscow, Kiev, Leningrad, Vilna, Minsk, and Tbilisi) wished to leave the Soviet Union, that they wished, as he wrote, to "seize an opportunity to flee the fear and discrimination which pursue them." He also reported—and stressed—that there was "no doubt" that Israel, the state that was then a mere eighteen years old, "occupies a vital and central place in the consciousness of Russian Jews at all ages and at all levels." As he wrote: "Jews are interested in news from Israel not simply out of curiosity but out of a profound sense of shared purpose. They feel that what happens there also affects them, that their fate is linked with that of the Jewish state. And if they still dream of a messianic future, it is because there, across the sea, an attempt has already been made to establish a third Temple, a third Jewish Commonwealth. From afar, in thought and silent prayer, they strive to take part in that endeavor."

It is very important to remember that when these words were written, Jews could not go from the Soviet Union to Israel. Even though the State of Israel had diplomatic relations with Russia, and there was an Israeli Legation in Moscow, the road from Moscow to Jerusalem was closed.

In June 1966, Elie Wiesel's book was ready for publication, and he had just written his preface "To the Reader." Six months later, in Paris, the Soviet prime minister, Alexei Kosygin, issued a formal declaration that Jews could, if they applied to do so, go to Israel to be reunited with members of their family. In that year, indeed, 2,027 exit visas had been granted. This change in Soviet practice electrified Soviet Jewry, rousing hopes which had hitherto been impossible even to contemplate.

In June 1967, just as those hopes were spreading throughout the cities of the Soviet Union, the verbal threats President Nasser of Egypt had unleashed against Israel were transformed into actual military preparations, in which both Syria and Jordan joined. The Jews of Moscow, like those throughout the world, watched with apprehension as the small state awaited the onslaught. Israel, endangered, struck first, destroying Egypt's air forces on the ground. Then the three Arab armies attacked. Radio Moscow, jubilant at the initial Arab successes in breaking across the 1949 cease-fire lines, announced the imminent destruction of the nineteen-year-old state.

This trumpeting of Israel's last hours of existence as a state released the hidden Jewishness and national pride of Russia's silent Jews. With each Radio Moscow broadcast of another Arab victory, fear for Israel's existence turned into a passionate longing to be a part of the struggle: "to die with my people," as one of those affected by the new awakening expressed it to me in Moscow sixteen years later.

"At first," another of my Moscow friends wrote to me, "it was the anguish at the thought that the Jews (I mean also Israel as an independent state) once again will be the victims." Then, several days after Soviet Jewry's instant and instinctive identity with an apparently defeated brother, the truth became known: Israel had driven back the invading armies.

Israel's victory gave Soviet Jews a clear, indisputable reason to be proud of being Jewish. With pride in Israel came a deep desire to make a personal contribution to the life and future of the Jewish state, a desire the Kosygin declaration of December 1966 seemed to bring within the bounds of reality. But no sooner had the Six Day War ended than the granting of exit visas came to a halt. All those who persisted in applying for exit visas were told that there was no chance of applications being granted as long as diplomatic relations with Israel, broken off in the war, were not restored.

The awakening of Soviet Jewry, however, could not be reversed by a political decision not to issue any further visas, and in the aftermath of the Israeli victory there was an upsurge of activity. The small Hebrew-language classes which had sprung up in the mid-1960s now burgeoned. Even larger meetings now took place at the sites of the mass murder of Jews by the Nazis during World War II. Private discussion groups exchanged information about Israeli life. The applications for exit visas continued, with hundreds of Soviet Jews trying to find relatives in Israel from whom an invitation could be sent—the formal invitation without which no visa application could even be begun.

Tens of thousands of Soviet Jews now embarked on an exhilarating, and for many an ultimately satisfactory, voyage: the road to Jewish identity, and then to Israel.

Beginning on a tiny scale in September 1967, and rising rapidly in the following four months, exit visas were granted to 379 Soviet citizens who had received the required formal "invitation" from Israel, authenticated as it had to be by an Israeli notary, and sent openly in the mail from Israel to the Soviet Union. Thousands of Soviet Jews now began to ask for these invitations, the first step in a long and complicated procedure. This procedure included the requirement that one obtain the permission of one's parents to leave. It also involved revealing to one's employer and local Party organization the intention to leave, thus risking—and normally losing—one's job.

The number of Jews (230) actually allowed to leave the Soviet Union in 1968 was lower than for any of the previous six years, almost the lowest since 1955. The impossibility of all but a tiny fraction of exit visas being granted, however, did not deter the awakening of Jewish national consciousness. In September 1968, at a memorial meeting at Babi Yar, the ravine in Kiev where more than 30,000 Jews had been massacred by the Nazis in a three-day orgy of killing in September 1941, Jews gathered in pious memorial. During the ceremony, the official Soviet speakers, while honoring the dead, also abused the State of Israel. Among the Jews present was a twenty-two-year-old student, Boris Kochubievsky. "What's going on here?" he heard a man ask. To which a woman replied, "Here the Germans killed a hundred thousand Jews." "That," commented the man, "was not enough." Boris Kochubievsky protested to the authorities. He had already applied to go to Israel and, to his surprise, on November 28, 1968, he received permission. Then, nine days later, he was arrested, held in prison for five months, and on May 13, 1969, brought to trial.

Kochubievsky was sentenced to three years in a labor camp. In his final remarks to the court, he expressed his hope "that no one else will share my fate because of his desire to go to Israel."

The sentence on Kochubievsky, with whom fourteen years later I walked across the hills south of Jerusalem, did not inhibit the aspirations of those Soviet Jews for whom the survival of the State of Israel during the Six Day War had been such an inspiration. That October, several thousand Jews gathered in Arkhipova Street in Moscow, outside the synagogue. It was the eve of Simchat Torah, the Jewish festival of the Rejoicing of the Law. In a quarter-mile section of the narrow street, these Jews, most of them between the ages of eighteen and twenty-four, sang and danced in the cold drizzle until late into the night. Some sang Yiddish songs; others took up the refrains in Hebrew, the language of the Jewish state. Some of those in the crowd had pieces of paper on which they had written out such words as they knew in modern Hebrew; avidly, these words were exchanged and spoken. One of the songs heard that night was a jingle mocking Soviet anti-Semitism.

When 1969 came to an end, it was clear that still no substantial emigration was to be allowed. Three thousand Jews received their exit visas during that single year, the largest number in any year since the days of the Communist Revolution of 1917. But that number was in sharp contrast to the thirty-four thousand who, in the sixteen months since September 1968, had asked for invitations from Israel.

On August 6, 1969, eighteen Jewish families from the Soviet republic of Georgia sent a letter to the United Nations Commission on Human Rights. They wrote proudly of "those who had handed down to us the tradition of struggle and faith," and ended with the appeal: "Let us go to the land of our forefathers." To the Israeli representative at the United Nations, Joseph Tekoah, these same Jewish families declared: "The time of fear is over—the time of action has come!"

Throughout the Soviet Union, Jews were beginning to demand the right to leave, or were becoming active in trying to learn about Jewish life and about the State of Israel. In February 1970, in the town of Ryazan, four Jews from the city's Institute of Radio Technology were sent to labor camps for encouraging young Jews to seek the path of Jewishness and emigration. One of them, Yury Vudka, was sentenced to seven years. Today he lives in Israel.

In March 1970, several Soviet newspapers published articles claiming that the Russian Jews did not wish to emigrate. In answer, forty Russian Jews wrote a letter, which was published abroad, stating that this was not true. Among the signatories was the forty-three-year-old Vladimir Slepak, the son of a devout Communist.

Jewish protests against these anti-emigration articles were widespread. On October 30, 1970, the trial took place in Kishinev of two Jews, Yakov Suslensky and Iosif Mishener, schoolteachers from the town of Bendery, in the Soviet republic of Moldavia. Their alleged "crime" was to have protested against one of the articles, this particular one in the Communist Party newspaper *Izvestia*, which maintained that no Jews wished to leave the Soviet Union for Israel. Both men were found guilty of anti-Soviet slander. Suslensky was sentenced to seven years in a labor camp and Mishener to six. Today, both of them live in Israel.

The number of exit visas fell during 1970, averaging less than eighty a month. At the same time, the number of Jews who had been refused an exit visa was growing. Among these Refuseniks, as they had become known, was a small group who, seeing no hope of having their refusals reversed, decided to seize a twelve-seat airplane and fly it to Sweden. They were caught and brought to trial in Leningrad. The main charge leveled against them was treason. Under Article 64A of the Criminal Code of the Russian republic, treason is punishable by death.

"All I wanted," one of the accused, Edward Kuznetsov, told the court, "was to live in Israel." But such protestations were to no avail. On December 24, 1970, the Leningrad sentences were made public. Two of the accused, Kuznetsov and Mark Dymshits, were sentenced to death, the rest to ten years and more in strict-regime labor camps. As the sentences were announced, their friends in the courtroom cried out: "Hold on! We are with you! We are waiting for you! We shall be in Israel together!"

Jews in the West were outraged by the harsh sentences. Outside the Supreme Court in Moscow, among several dozen Russian Jews who gathered in protest, was Elena Bonner, a relative of Edward Kuznetsov. During the demonstration she met another of the protesters, Dr. Andrei Sakharov, a member of the Soviet Academy of Sciences and a non-Jew. Six weeks earlier, Dr. Sakharov had been among the founders of the courageously named Soviet Committee on Human Rights, offering what it called "creative help" to any Soviet citizens who might need a safeguard for their human rights, as defined by the Universal Declaration of Human Rights of 1948.

As Western protests grew, the two death sentences were commuted to fifteen years in prison and labor camp. Even these harsh sentences did not deter other Jews from continuing their public demands for exit visas, despite the fact that only 1,044 Jews had been allowed out in 1970.

Two months after the Leningrad trial, a conference was convened by the Israeli government and Jewish community leaders from throughout the Western world. Opening in Brussels on February 23, 1971, and later known as "Brussels One," the conference called on the Soviet government to give exit visas to any Jews who wished to go to Israel. Eight days before the conference opened, the Soviet news agency Tass had already condemned it as an "anti-Soviet provocation." At Brussels, Elie Wiesel was among those who spoke out for Jews in Russia. "I saw them dancing," he said. "I saw them dancing on Simchat Torah, and that dancing changed my life."

On February 26, 1971, while the Brussels conference was still in session, twenty-four Jews marched to the visa office in Riga and demanded the right to leave. Their public protest—a rarity in the Soviet Union and an act of considerable courage—was followed two days later by a "sit-in" outside the Supreme Soviet in Moscow by thirty Jews who, in the previous months, had been refused their exit visas.

The Supreme Soviet protest of February 28, 1971, was followed within three weeks by the announcement of a second trial, also to be held in Leningrad, which opened on May 11. Nine

Jews were brought to trial, two of them accused of treason, including a young Hebrew teacher, Hillel Butman, who had been active in the growing emigration movement. Butman was sentenced to ten years in a strict-regime labor camp. Then, on May 24, a third trial opened, this time in Riga. It was in Riga, the capital of the Latvian republic, that many Jews gathered each year at the wartime mass-murder pits at Rumbuli to remember the dead and to renew their sense of Jewish identity.

One of the four Riga Jews accused was a twenty-three-year-old nurse, Ruth Alexandrovich. She was charged with distributing six copies of a small, privately prepared brochure, *For the Return of Soviet Jews to their Homeland*, and fifteen copies of a second brochure, *Your Native Tongue*, on the Hebrew language. "In the Soviet newspapers," Ruth Alexandrovich told the court, "they write with bias against Israel." She had intended to correct that bias. "In the Soviet Union there are no Jewish schools." Her advocacy of Hebrew was intended to fill that gap. She was sentenced to a year in a labor camp.

Today, both Hillel Butman and Ruth Alexandrovich live in Israel.

On May 20, 1971, in a gesture of sympathy in response to the growing harassment of Jews, Academician Sakharov's Committee on Human Rights appealed in an open letter to the Supreme Soviet about the "persecution of Jewish repatriates." The "only aim" of those on trial, the committee said, was to "protest against the unlawful refusals to give them visas for repatriation."

The decade that had opened with such courageous protests was to see a miracle: the emigration before the end of that decade of a quarter of a million Soviet Jews. Nearly two-thirds went to Israel; just over a third went to the United States. Those who went to Israel formed one of the largest mass immigration movements in Israel's history. Then, in 1980, the gates began to close. More than 350,000 Jews who had sought the essential "invitation" from Israel were trapped. Also trapped were more than 12,000 Jews who had managed to acquire all the documents needed to apply for an exit visa, but had been refused. These were the Refuseniks. As of

1986, some have continued to be denied permission to leave over a period of more than fifteen years. They include Vladimir Slepak, one of the authors of the courageous protest of March 1970.

When Elie Wiesel wrote *The Jews of Silence*, we in the West did not know even the names of those trapped Jews. No links for obtaining this information existed. His book was a miracle of contact. As a survivor of the Holocaust, he understood what it meant to be forgotten, and what it meant to be a witness. It was not until 1976 that the shocking fact reached the West from the Soviet Union that there were as many as *five hundred* Jewish families who had been refused their exit visas. This information reached London, New York, and Jerusalem in a series of lists typed on flimsy paper (I have a set of them in front of me as I write these words).

It was these disturbing lists that first gave the names and addresses of those Jews known to be "in refusal." Suddenly, the Jews ceased to be anonymous. The lists had been compiled in Moscow by a number of Jewish activists, among them Dr. Alexander Lunts and Dina Beilina, both of whom now live in Israel. The lists achieved public prominence in 1978, when Anatoly Shcharansky was accused by the KGB of being their principal compiler. Dozens of Soviet Jews were interrogated about the compilation of these lists: how had their names got on them? How had the lists reached the West?

Since 1978, when Shcharansky was given a savage thirteen-year sentence, other brave Soviet Jews have continued to send lists of Refuseniks to the West. It is as a result of their bravery that we know today that more than *twelve thousand* Jews have been refused their exit visas (a twenty-four-fold increase over 1976). The gates of emigration, through which 250,000 Jews passed in the "miracle" decade of the 1970s, are to all intents and purposes closed. Those gates are particularly harshly shut against the Jews who have been Refuseniks longest, including more than a hundred of those whose names appear on the original lists of 1976: among them, Vladimir Prestin, Pavel Abramovich, and Yuly

Kosharovsky, leaders of the Jewish movement in the 1970s, and now, in the second half of the 1980s, still denied their wish to live in Israel. Another of those on the original lists of a decade ago is Professor Alexander Lerner, now aged seventy-three. Last year I dedicated my book *The Holocaust* to him. Two of his daughters, then little girls, were murdered by the Nazis in 1941; his third daughter awaits him in Israel.

To be a Refusenik is to be isolated and alone in Soviet society, often harassed, pilloried, denounced, and even in danger of arrest. As I write these words, more than twenty Soviet Jews are in prison or a labor camp for their part in the struggle for emigration. These include Dr. Iosif Begun, sentenced in October 1983 (after almost a year in prison awaiting trial) to twelve years. This was Dr. Begun's third sentence in less than a decade.

Among the twenty Jewish prisoners are several Hebrew teachers, including Leonid Volvovsky from Gorki and Alec Zelichenok from Leningrad, both sentenced to three years in a labor camp. On June 9, 1986, as the world speculated on the date and eventual outcome of the next Reagan–Gorbachev summit, yet another Hebrew teacher, Alexei Magarik (a twenty-seven-year-old cellist) was sentenced to three years in a labor camp. His father lives in Israel; his wife, Natalia, looks after their infant son, Chaim, in Moscow.

For several of the prisoners, the years 1985 and 1986 saw an upsurge inside the labor camps of physical violence and severe injuries, illnesses untreated, and appeals for clemency ignored. Western campaigners for Soviet Jewry were particularly shocked by such cruelties—especially the near blinding of Iosif Berenstein and the accidental crippling of Yuly Edelstein, who was subsequently denied medical attention.

Anatoly Shcharansky, whose release from prison in February 1986 delighted not only campaigners for Soviet Jewry but the whole Western world, was fortunate (and indeed blessed) that throughout his nine years in prison and labor camp his wife, Avital, campaigned tirelessly for him throughout the free world. Hers was often an uphill struggle, but she never faltered. Unfortunately, none of the other prisoners has a wife in the West to campaign as she did for him. Each must therefore depend entirely upon the good will, energy, and initiative of ordinary men and women around the world.

Isolated as they are in the labor-camp zones of the Ural Mountains, or of even remoter Siberia, many of the Jewish prisoners are sustained by their wives who, from inside the Soviet Union, nevertheless do their utmost to inform the West of their plight: by letter, through telephone calls, and through visitors. Few things are more important, as a practical measure of support, than for Western Jews—writers, teachers, attorneys, community leaders—to go to the Soviet Union and to meet the wives of Jews who are in prison. How vividly I recall my own meetings with Dr. Begun's wife, Ina, with Leonid Volvovsky's wife, Mila, and with Alec Zelichenok's wife, Galina. These three women deserve—as do every prisoner's wife and family—all the support the West can give, either by visiting them in the Soviet Union or by championing their cause in the parliaments of the democratic world, from the Knesset to Capitol Hill.

As well as the twenty Jewish prisoners, there are more than twenty former prisoners who, although their sentences are over, are still refused exit visas. These include Vladimir Slepak, one of the longest of the long-term Refuseniks; Ida Nudel, who for almost a decade struggled to alert the world to the plight of all imprisoned Jews; and Dr. Victor Brailovsky, whose scientific seminar served, a decade ago, as one of the main centers of Jewish cultural identity in Moscow. Anatoly Shcharansky mentioned each of these former prisoners during his inspiring address on May 11, 1986 (Solidarity Sunday) in New York. His concern is widely echoed.

Every Jew who visits the Soviet Union is inspired to see how those Soviet Jews who have sought to emigrate, but have been refused permission to do so, form among themselves such a dedicated band of brothers. Theirs is not a selfish struggle but a common one. They rejoice in the few successes (all too few at the moment) and look to us in the West, and above all to Israel, to procure something better for them in the future. Their need is desperate now. So few long-term Refuseniks have been released in the last few years that statistically it would take several hundred years before an exit visa was granted to most of those who remain—a time span which is not even anticipated by the age-old Jewish wish: "Until 120." Not always recalled when making the wish is that this ideal age span was the age of Moses when he died—bitterly ironic too, in the context of Soviet Jewry, because Moses never entered the Promised Land, but could only see it from afar. "I know now," remarked a Leningrad Jew who has been a Refusenik for sixteen years, "that they have stolen my life."

The many hundreds of Soviet Jews who have been waiting twelve years and more for an exit visa have watched, at times with despair, the passing of the years inevitably reduce the time and energy they hoped to give to the land of Israel. Forced at the moment of applying for visas to leave their professions in the Soviet Union, they have been denied not only their visas, but also their wish to contribute, while still young, to life in the Jewish state. In March 1983, I myself was impressed by the way so many long-term Refuseniks had retained their hope of an eventual exit visa. But when I returned in August 1985, one of those whose hopes had so impressed me earlier remarked: "The hope you ascribe to us is very tenuous now."

Cruelly, it is often those who are strongest in their desire to go to Israel, and nowhere else, who have been held longest "in refusal": captives for an ideal which has led so many of them to absorb (while still behind the Iron Curtain) every aspect of Israeli life, and, above all, mastery of the language of Israel. It is not by chance that a majority of today's Prisoners of Zion are Hebrew teachers. We (Jews throughout the world, Zionists, and lovers of Israel, as well as Israelis) are all the more beholden, therefore, to campaign for them whenever we can: noisily in public, subtly in private, and persistently at all times. Above all, to know their names, and to name those names. To know their stories, and to make those stories an integral part of the diplomacy of the superpowers. Ignorance, like silence, cannot help them. As one Hebrew teacher and long-term Refusenik wrote to me from Moscow recently: "I don't see any progress in *aliyah*,* either in general or in our private case. But to my mind *now* is the time of decision here in Moscow on our issue. So it is extremely important now to concentrate all efforts."

By 1986 there were more than 12,000 Refuseniks, and as many as 360,000 Russian Jews (out of a total Jewish population of about two million) who had already sought the initial "invitation" from Israel to begin the process of application, despite the present hopelessness of such a path. Neither the 360,000 nor the still-silent majority of Russian Jews (whose silence is not necessarily eternal) are waiting for a new voice, like that of Theodor Herzl of old, to urge the modern pharaoh to "let my people go."

On November 22, 1984, a few months before his arrest, Alec Zelichenok wrote a letter to a friend in the West (it was one of the letters cited in his trial, as part of the accusation which led to a three-year sentence). "The young generation of our people here," Zelichenok wrote, "not only as a rule do not know anything of Jewish history, culture, traditions, but even do not suspect that such things exist. Their Jewishness gives them only troubles, converts them into third-rate citizens."

Zelichenok's letter continued: "We do our best to give them at least the elements, but the results are hardly visible. No wonder: for instance, there are less than 1,000 active Jews in Leningrad, with its 150,000 'official' Jews and about the same number of 'unofficial.' Seeing this percentage and the well-known circumstances of our existence, we have to recognize that our efforts are insufficient."

The courageous and far-sighted Zelichenok went on to raise the fear of all Soviet Jewish activists. "If the process of forced assimilation continues with the same speed, a new version of the final solution to the Jewish problem will come true here in some ten years, and if they let us go the process will even hasten." This was a pessimistic conclusion, but also, he and his friends believe, a realistic one. They do not intend to abandon hope, however. In

*Emigration to Israel.—*ed.*

spite of "the hard reality," Zelichenok concluded, "it would be too early to give up. 'It is still not midnight,' as they say in Russia. Not every avenue has been explored."

The Jewish activists in the Soviet Union, those who bear the brunt of the struggle, appeal to the Jews of the West to raise their voices in support of a reopening of the gates and on behalf of those who, like Zelichenok, have been punished for their legitimate aspirations. Not every Jew who can do so is prepared to answer that call. There are, however, noble exceptions. At the time of the arrest of the Hebrew teacher Leonid Volvovsky in 1985, his wife, Mila, appealed to Jewish writers and religious leaders in the West to demand her husband's release. Among those who answered her call was Elie Wiesel, in an article in the *New York Times* on October 22, 1985. "When Ronald Reagan meets Mikhail S. Gorbachev," he wrote, "I hope he will speak to him, among other things, of an innocent man who is now in danger of being sentenced to hard labor in the Soviet Union. His name is Leonid Volvovsky. He is a 45-year-old mathematician, and his trial opened last Friday in Gorki."

Leonid Volvovsky had first applied for an exit visa in 1976. Since then, as Elie Wiesel wrote, he had become "an outsider," the lot of all Refuseniks. "Overnight they are cut off, isolated, marked for harassment, abandoned by colleagues and humiliated by institutions. Still, they lean on each other and help each other to safeguard their sanity and morale." The Refuseniks, Elie Wiesel added, "are our heroes. They place their hope on us, on our involvement."

In his article, Elie Wiesel urged the Soviet leader to make a gesture on Volvovsky's behalf. "Will he make it?" he asked. "Should he do so, the Refusenik's hope in us may be justified and our hope in him as well."

These hopes proved (in the short term, at least) illusory. Three days after Elie Wiesel's article was published, Leonid Volvovsky was sentenced to three years in a labor camp.

When, on February 11, 1986, the Soviet authorities released Anatoly Shcharansky, it was Mila Volvovsky who sent a telegram to Jerusalem on behalf of the Refuseniks and the remaining twenty Jewish prisoners, including her husband. "Your heroism, Tolya, gave us strength to live during these long years," she wrote. "Our happiness today is endless."

Mila Volvovsky's joy was real. But her anguish is also real, as her husband remains (I write these words on July 4, 1986), a prisoner. "We must never forget," he wrote her from a labor camp on April 23, 1986, the eve of Passover, "that we were slaves in Egypt and that God freed us from bondage with a strong hand and an outstretched arm. Moreover, many nations have sought to subdue us in every generation, but the Holy One, blessed be He, has always saved us from our oppressors."

The revolution that took place after Elie Wiesel wrote *The Jews of Silence* was a formidable one. A quarter of a million Jews were able to go from darkness to light. Yet, with the gates now closed once more, the words of his pioneering book are as meaningful as they were twenty years ago: "I returned from the Soviet Union disheartened and depressed. But what torments me most is not the Jews of silence I met in Russia, but the silence of the Jews I live among today."

Thanks to Elie Wiesel's own writing and the work of hundreds of campaigners for Soviet Jewry throughout the free world, that Western silence is no longer what it was, a pitiful gap in Jewish unity. But the silence is still there, pierced from time to time by a murmur and on occasion by a shout, but not yet shattered, as it could be, by the sustained indignation of which the Jewish world is capable.

Surely it is possible to end once and for all the tragedy and the indignity of two million Jewish men, women, and children trapped behind a border which, however much they wish to cross it, cannot be crossed at will. It is quite wrong that they should be trapped in this way: two million human wrongs in an age that pays such loud lip service to promoting human rights. Surely our voice can and must be even louder, to open those gates again.

Nothing could be more timely than the reissuing of Elie

Wiesel's book, to remind us of the days when fear and hope seemed to have no outlet but despair, but when Israel, then as now, was a beacon in the darkness. Let all of us work today, as Elie Wiesel worked then, and still works, to provide our fellow Jews in the Soviet Union with a voice, and a mechanism, capable of leading out all who wish to go there—to the Jewish state which once, in 1940 (when needed most), did not exist, but which to-day, as a sovereign state, waits with an open border and an eager heart.

Merton College, Oxford
July 4, 1986